Auntie June,
   with much love and thanks
for your support and
sponsorship.
   Richard

      xx

Safe, Happy, Fast

by

Richard Parson

This book is published by
Grosvenor House Publishing Ltd
28–30 High Street, Guildford, Surrey, GU1 3HY.
www.grosvenorhousepublishing.co.uk

A CIP record for this book
is available from the British Library

Printed in Great Britain by Biddles Ltd, Kings Lynn, Norfolk

ISBN 1-905529-62-7

Foreword

Safe, happy and fast asleep at my desk, I was extremely flattered to be asked by Richard to write a foreword to his book describing his experiences on Team Stelmar, given that so many people, from 'famous round the world yachtsman' Sir Chay Blyth, to skipper Clive Cosby and all the other crew that actually sailed in the race, are clearly more qualified than the plain old sponsor's project manager. But then it dawned on me that all those sailors have plenty of experience of trying to condense the emotions of a lifetime into one small page through providing the daily logs written on board. They must've all run away screaming when Richard caught their eye. So you got me.

Stelmar was not a particularly large company to be signing up for this venture, and the fact is we matched the Crew Volunteers' amateur status pound for pound in the early stages of the project, the mandate landing with a thud on my desk to form a project team of, um, one, whilst also tackling my day job as Chartering Manager for our fleet of 40 oil tankers. But if the crew formerly known as Team Seven had less than average luck in the sponsorship sweepstakes, we at Stelmar plucked first prize in two draws. First, we were fortunate enough to engage the services of Valeria Sesto, Clive's wife, to act as Ports Manager (and just-about-everything-else Manager), who showed us quickly which end was up in the sailing and sponsorship world, and second, we ended up with the best skipper and crew in the fleet. They all combined to make their sponsors look remarkably good, and have my undying gratitude.

Being such a small shore team – the entire Stelmar London office was just four persons - gave us one advantage over our rivals, in that we got to know the crew as individuals very quickly and often very closely. And Richard was one of the first stand-outs from the crowd: because of his career as an undertaker; his witty log writing that won the first Rubber Chicken Award on Leg1 and our chats when sharing beers and a plane back from BA as he sorted out his US Visa. But mostly because he's even more bald than I am.

The crew lost their amateur tag quite early in the race, their sponsors a bit later, probably a day or two before we got taken over and the Stelmar name disappeared from everywhere in the world except the sides of a 72ft yacht and her sails. You are about to read a story of amazing resilience and determination in overcoming everything the world and his girlfriend could think of to throw at Richard, and much of it had a spooky resonance here as we endured being served up as a tasty snack in the sushi bar that is Wall Street. On January 20th the boat was on the other side of the world, with just 15 crew remaining out of 18, and her sponsor was history. What happened next? Turn the page and find out.

For Richard and me it's back to the day job. I only hope his work didn't pile up whilst he was away like mine did.

David Chapman
London, July 2005

"The moving finger writes; and having writ moves on. Nor all thy piety nor wit can lure it back to cancel one half line. Nor all thy tears wash out a word of it."

Omar Kyhham

On a cold, wet and windy day, the 3rd October 2004 at 2.00pm G.M.T. the starting gun for the 2004/5 Global Challenge Yacht Race was fired by Her Royal Highness, the Princess Royal from Southsea Castle in Portsmouth, England.

Under the canopy of umbrellas alongside her, amidst the raincoats and plastic bags which had been hastily utilized as protective wear against the wind and the rain, the shouts and cheers of thousands rang out.

Every single one of them were mesmerized by the twelve identical steel yachts which jostled for position before their very eyes, each yacht desperate to be the first away on their thirty-six thousand mile yacht race.

Team Stelmar was first across the line.

The roar from well wishers mingled with the wind and the rain and was virtually unheard by the two hundred crew volunteers that crewed the fleet of racing yachts.

So far, we had travelled a long way on our mental journey, but this was the dawning of the day as far as I was concerned.

Here, real life took over from our careers and we had to learn to apply the lessons of not only the last few months and years, but of a whole lifetime.

We also had to learn new lessons and they sometimes weren't easy to learn, nor were they always easy to teach.

We sailed down the Solent in the rain, with twenty knots of wind from the south-west, into the short, grey seas and the murky afternoon.

The twelve yachts, that were to be home for us all during the next ten months, passed the Isle of Wight and then the Needles as the spectator craft finally headed back and left us on our own.

We sailed on to race each other around the planet, across its desolate, lonely and unforgiving oceans.

For some of the crews, this was the realization of childhood dreams, for others a new opportunity for adventure which they grasped with both hands.

The shouts, cheers and tears of those nearest and dearest, got washed away in the wind and the rain.

The adventure had begun.

It was fantastic.

In the beginning.....

The London Boat show on January 17th 2004, held for the first time at London's Excel Centre, Docklands, was the scheduled venue for the Crew Announcements.

This was scheduled to be the official Global Challenge announcement, eight months before the race start date, where the individual crew volunteers were told which other individuals they would be sailing with, to make up the crews for the 2004/5 Global Challenge Yacht Race.

We waited all day.

It was a significant moment for all of us.

I had been training for four years for this moment.

After all this time, I was to be placed into a specific race team at last.

The decisions and selections had been made, all that was needed now was to let the crews know.

I just didn't know many of the other people in the room, some of whom I would be depending on completely for the next year of my life, in the world's most trying conditions.

The Skipper Announcements had been made at the beginning of November at Saint Katharine's Dock, London and their individual profiles had appeared in various yachting press and media.

The world had largely missed the *Skipper Announcements* but they were significant for us crew volunteers.

Twelve skippers and two reserves had been chosen from three hundred and fifty applicants.

It was true that the guys that had been through the Challenge training schedule were well represented, but there were one or two other pedigree skippers peppered in.

Some of them were better qualified than others.

We were about to be told which skippers we would be sailing with.

Chay Blyth was going to announce which crew volunteers would be sailing with which skippers to make up the teams.

Hundreds attended and wearing our yellow blouson jackets provided by Challenge Business, we waited anxiously for the news.

At 6.00pm G.M.T. we all assembled in an upstairs conference room and were served drinks.

At approximately 8.00pm, slightly later than intended, Sir Chay said a few words of encouragement, namely: "Don't ask!"

The decisions had been made.

There were to be no options for asking to be moved into a different team, for any reason whatsoever.

Take it or leave it.

It was an anxious moment.

The twelve skippers made their way to various points across the room and made themselves obvious.

When grouped, we were to make our way towards our skippers.

Some of the yachts already had individual sponsors which was a load off the crews' minds so far as help with the cost of foul weather clothing, food and provisions, accommodation and information in stop-over ports was concerned. Together with the thousand and one other things that we needed to pay for, but hadn't included in the original budget.

Those teams that were still *Sponsor Pending* would just get a number at the moment.

Sponsor Pending as a worse case scenario, could mean that we should expect no financial help from any future sponsor and we would have to raise all the costs ourselves, estimated to be another twenty thousand pounds on top of the twenty-seven thousand pounds that we had already paid to Challenge Business to get this far.

The names started to appear on an O.H.P.

The seventh team announced included my name.

Team Seven was born.

Nicko Brennan, Matt Petersen, Jonathan Rabley, Phil Beck, Julian Smith, Mike Morgan, Alex Alley, Newton Scott, Tim "Flash" Johnston, Richard Parson, Paul Goodman, Sarah Lamb, Kate Stainsby, Susan Lyons and Ruth Newton with Clive Cosby as Skipper.

People are often categorized by what they do for a living.

I don't buy into that, but for your information, with my descriptions added where I feel appropriate, they were as follows;

Nicko was a computer programmer and the brains behind the operation.

Matt was a policeman, about to be promoted.

Jonathan was a 'businessman'. (I don't know what he did, to be honest.)

Phil was an airport baggage handling systems operator and the brawn, liberally sprinkled with large doses of common sense, technical knowledge and huge doses of human tolerance, in our machine.

Julian was a project manager with a fair understanding of yacht racing and sail trim. He also had a very subtle sense of humour, which took me some time to tune in to, but was actually very concise and clever.

Mike was not working, having semi-retired as a computer programmer. He had competed in the first leg of the last race, as well as completed many miles in the Challenge yachts, which helped us in the early stages, but he wasn't really a sailor.

Alex was, is and always will be a boat bum, never happier than when he was afloat. He was a great bloke to have around and very useful in many aspects. Although he was useful from the start, after the first leg Alex's personality on Team Stelmar came much more to the fore and he became a fundamental member of the team.

Newton was a non-executive company director who was doing the race to raise money for Breakthrough Breast Cancer.

Flash was an accountant but he wasn't telling his employers about his decision to take part in the race as yet. He still got in all the photos for the website and for prosperity so that I had to doctor them before I was able to post them. He was a big, strong guy that caught my attention by wearing a T-shirt that read 'It takes a big guy to cry … but a bigger one to make him.'

I'm a funeral director. *'Unapproachable, Argumentative and Fiery'*… reportedly.

Paul was an HGV driver who had sold the family scrap metal business and wasn't 'just a driver'. There's drivers and there's drivers, eh Paul? Paul was also very technical.

Sarah was a student.

Kate was a physiotherapist and organised everyone and everything. With her personable way, she could often convince you that she was right or at least talk you into going along with her.

Susan was a P.A., previously a ballet dancer. She saw things that I could never see.

Ruth was a doctor, having qualified recently. She had signed up for the race when I did, four years ago, when she was still a student.

Clive was the professional and he had a reasonable pedigree in yacht racing. His strengths, as well as ours developed as we continued on our voyage.

With the exception of Nicko, who was Australian, and Jonathan who was an American, we all lived in the U.K. at that stage.

So now you know us!

Most of us were in full time occupations, still trying to raise the money to pay for our Berth Fees.

We would be quitting work in a few months and as a team, we had no financial backing.

It seemed like we had a big job ahead all of a sudden.

I got spooked.

My fiancée, Tina, was waiting with my family and friends as well as the many other crew volunteers' friends and family, at the main hall for the announcements to be flashed up on the computer screen on the Challenge Stand.

I sent her a text message.

"Oh No!"

Somehow, I found myself hating the moment.

It was like being the new boy at school on the first day. Everybody else seemed to know one another, because most of them had only recently completed their training, or were still doing it. I had completed mine two years ago. Since then, most of my training had been off my own back or on cross channel races in friends' boats.

I felt like I didn't belong there.

Instead of making my way straight over to my skipper and my team, I headed in the opposite direction to the toilets and washed my face under the running tap and took a few deep breaths. The cold water was intended to shake me up and put some colour back into my cheeks, as well as giving me the opportunity to compose myself.

As I headed back into the room to join my new crew it became obvious that the water wasn't cold enough, nor my breaths deep enough.

One of the Challenge staff stopped me.

"Are you okay?" she asked
"Yes, I'm fine" I replied unconvincingly
"Are you sure?" she persisted

I mumbled something incoherent in a futile attempt to convince her, brushed her by and carried on walking to the corner of the room.

I wasn't disappointed with my team mates, I didn't really know them and I wasn't comfortable with that. I had met Clive on one of my first training sails and had obviously watched his progress on the Challenge Business Round Britain and Ireland Race the previous year, which I had also taken part in and he had done well.

He certainly came from a racing background, which was what I wanted.

I think that the realization that the race was now almost upon me, together with the facts that I had my eye on two or three of the other skippers, I didn't know any of my team mates and we had no money, unsettled me.

They all seemed to be laughing and joking together, thick as thieves so as to speak, I was standing on the periphery looking in.

I didn't get their humour and I felt like I was outside of myself watching events unfold.

Square peg, round hole.

I met Clive and the team and I was handed a polo shirt, which I hastily hoisted over my shoulders before making my way, together with the rest of the team, to a photographer in the corner of the room where we had our first team photograph taken.

Not all the crew volunteers were able to attend the event for various reasons, but those of us that were there stood in formation and smiled.

After our first photographs we had our first team outing. An Argentinean restaurant had been booked for our first meal together, in recognition of our first stopover port.

Our first tactical movements showed a weakness though as we first headed for a taxi rank, then a bus queue, before returning to the taxi rank and travelling via a combination of both means of transport in unorganized disarray.

I don't remember the journey back to the accommodation later that night, but when I woke the next morning, I had a hang-over and I wasn't completely delighted with my lot.

Following breakfast, Tina and I headed for Gatwick Airport and the flight back to Plymouth. As we flew over Dartmouth and Salcombe in Devon, I gazed out of the window and thought about the Sunday morning sailing I was missing in Plymouth.

It was the morning after the night before and I wasn't happy.

I couldn't help but feel that I had missed out.

I thought that I would be elated but I wasn't.

I didn't know what was bothering me, but something was really eating away at me from the inside.

I hadn't bargained on feeling slightly deflated.

When I arrived back in Plymouth Airport, the world looked different somehow.

I knew that I was on the verge of something massive, but I didn't know what exactly.

It was a really strange notion to be carrying around in my head and I couldn't sleep at night.

I looked out of the window instead and stared at the moon in a kind of trance. I tried to imagine what was to come and how I was going to deal or cope with it.

The trouble was I had no idea what was going to happen next, let alone know how to deal with it.

I had been sailing in dinghies and keel boats for many years, but in specific preparation for this race, I had taken my education to a more formal level with night-school classes and weekend courses as well as more specific practical sail training.

I had passed my RYA Yachtmaster theory exams, got my Radio Operators licence and my RYA First Aiders certificate and I had sailed approximately eight thousand miles of offshore sailing, including the Challenge Business Round Britain and Ireland Race in 2003.

I had sailed more than twenty thousand miles in various boats, including local club racing, National Championships, European Championships and even on one occasion, had qualified and taken part as crew in the J24 World Championships in Genoa, Italy by coming third in the UK J24 National Championships.

I had maintained a strict fitness/training programme for the previous three years and had swapped my company car for a bicycle to increase my fitness and stamina levels and attending a gym and fitness classes three or four times a week.

I had also, after a lifetime's commitment, given up smoking.

I wanted to be coupled with someone that had an ocean racing pedigree and learn to race across the world's oceans. I was eager to go sailing with a professional skipper and with a professional team.

I threw myself into the Team Seven ethos, such as I understood it to be. But it gradually dawned on me that not everyone was as committed as I was.

I probably just needed some reassurance that what I was doing was right.

As it turned out, I think that I was too enthusiastic.

Within a matter of days, Clive forwarded an e-mail to the team from Matt Petersen; he had had an opportunity for promotion at work and had decided to take it.

He quit the team.

Next to go was Jonathan Rabley.

Jonathan lived and worked in America, he had already withdrawn his intention to race but the message hadn't got through.

Clive was having a difficult job in catching up with him to say 'Hello' and welcome him to the team through his work contact number and e-mail address and after several unsuccessful attempts he was eventually able to get through on his home phone number.

The subsequent conversation reportedly went something like this;

"Hi, this is Jonathan Rabley"
"Johnathan, Hi! This is Clive Cosby, the skipper of Team Seven."
"Eek!"

Brrrrrrrrrrrr

The line went dead.

Subsequent attempts at contacting him were unsuccessful, eventually Clive reported his experience to the Challenge administration staff who relayed the fact that John had withdrawn and would not be taking part.

Two crew members down, after as many weeks.

The Team Seven Monster rumbled to life and things began to happen.

The first thing that we did was to organize a weekly telephone conference call, a routine that continued right up until the week prior to race week.

Julian sorted it out and on Monday evenings at 2000 hours initially, we had a business meeting and many smaller sub-committees began the immense task of organizing a round the world yacht race. The 6 digit password for entry to our "Room" was 777777.

We were all on time for the calls.

That was a good sign.

The team website went live at the beginning of February but we didn't establish the name Team Seven until just after that, so on 10th February, it became *www.7eam.com* thanks to Nicko, who also organized our personal e-mail addresses, with various group addresses for relevant working parties (i.e. weather group or technical clothing etc.) all with lots of 7eam's and 7's.

It wasn't long before some articles started to appear on the website, together with crew profiles and individuals' photographs.

We began to establish an identity and it felt good.

We were still skint though.

We each had to pay £100 for our team building weekends, which were as regularly as we could organize them, we had to pay over £3,000 for insurance, we had to take as many days leave as we could possibly get away with whilst still giving the impression of being at work, we had to call in as many favours and kind gestures as we possibly could from family and friends, the project immediately took over my whole life and the lives of those nearest to me.

Pretty much overnight.

When we attended the first 7eam team building session on Friday 6th February, we met up at the Hayling Island Sailing Club. It was scheduled to run from Friday 6th through until Sunday 8th.

Most us were able to turn up on Friday and were therefore installed in time to be woken at 0600 hours on Saturday morning with Clive poking a video camera at us before being taken on a physical training session.

Leading these sessions was Valeria Sesto, Clive's Argentinian wife.

Vale is a personal fitness trainer so she went straight to work on assessing our individual levels of fitness and writing out training programmes for us. Vale also had a background in sailing both dinghies and the Challenge yachts so was able to concentrate on exactly the right individual training programmes for us.

She was totally committed to the team right from the start and absolutely invaluable to us from the very first days. Her dedication to the whole project however, coupled with some language differences meant that she was occasionally misunderstood by different people that we encountered.

Her dedication helped us out time and time again.

After that first session we showered and headed for the dining area for breakfast. Although the facilities at the club included a first class kitchen and food preparation area, the cooked breakfasts that were on offer to the club members were off the menu for Team Seven. Vale had pre-instructed the staff on exactly what we were to eat and more importantly, what we were not to eat.

Three times over the course of that weekend, members of the kitchen staff apologized to me for the food that they were serving.

I actually thought that the food was good, but our menu was strict and they had received instructions.

The competitive edge that some of us had as character traits began to make an appearance when we enjoyed a game of touch rugby during Friday afternoon. Mike Morgan demonstrated his enthusiasm to the team when he couldn't stop his one time charge to the water's edge, which ended with him swimming in the oggin. The rugby ball that he was chasing however, didn't escape him so I suppose that you could say that the charge was successful.

We all came home with various cuts, bruises and strains after that first team build and the injury list grew with each subsequent occasion, later prompting some concern from Clive that he was gradually putting the entire team out of action. His fears were allayed slightly, but the injuries kept on coming.

The result of that first weekend though, after some classroom work and expectation analysis (get me!) had us come up with the ethos of what we wanted to achieve on this race.

Collectively, we wanted to be Safe, Happy and Fast.

The second team-building weekend took place on the 12th – 14th March 2004 and once again it was held at the Hayling Island Sailing Club.

Mike Morgan lived in Dorset, I had phoned him before the first team build and offered to pick him up. He and I drove one another to nearly all of our team-building sessions, we talked quite a lot. He had sailed a bit in the Challenge yachts and taken part in the first leg of the last race. He complained about a lot, but was basically fairly communicative and relayed his life view or perspective to me as we drove up and back from the Portsmouth and Southampton all summer.

He was a country boy really.

Quiet, strong and a bit of a loner, who liked his beer.

I was fond of Mike.

I picked him up from Dorset for the second team build and together we collected Rob Hooykaas from Southampton Airport.

Rob was a new member of the team, having been just announced to us by Clive via the weekly conference call.

I had e-mailed him a photo of loads of CV's (crew volunteers), taken at the London Boat Show, with us all wearing our yellow jackets and looking identical, so that he would recognize us at the airport.

He had no trouble finding us.

Rob lives in Holland with his lovely wife Peggy. It was his first introduction. He had been on the reserve crew list and had been placed with us to replace one of the crew that had quit.

He is a strongly built guy with a relaxed manner, an infectious smile and is not backwards in coming forwards.

I instantly took a liking to Rob and later Peggy too.

My report of the weekend for the Team Seven website went as follows:

For our second team-building weekend, we returned to the excellent facilities of the Hayling Island Sailing Club.

This weekend started at the earlier time of 1200 hours. Shortly before "TB2" kicked off, we met our new team member Robert Hooykaas.

Robert signed up for the challenge over a year ago. He was actually placed with "7eam" at the beginning of February, but, due to a prior engagement, he couldn't be named until now. Robert's profile and photograph will appear quite soon.

Robert's addition to the team was accompanied by Nicko's first public appearance. Nicko literally rolled in on his scooter. He has been in at the very start of Team Seven, although having been in Australia made for some slight difficulties. Nicko, who is the creator of our website, stood out immediately by texting us from Sydney, live at the crew announcements to say how pleased he was to be a part of the team.

Our invited guests this weekend were a follows;

Vale Sesto

Vale takes care of us from the inside. She is advising the team on Nutrition and Diet, as well as Physical Training and Fitness. She competed in the 2000/1 B.T. Global Challenge and with her wealth of experience, is an invaluable member of the team. She is also great at scaring chefs!

Cian McCarthy

Cian will be helping with Weather, Routing and Currents. His Challenge sailing experience has been as navigator/tactician aboard LG Flatron in the

2000/1 B.T. Global Challenge, the overall race winners. Along with his vast wealth of sailing experience, he was welcomed to the team.

Dr. Wil James Ph.D

Wil is also responsible for taking care of us inside. He is a sports psychologist who will be helping us with the mental preparation and winning focus required by top sportsmen & women. Reportedly, Wil is a stretch, not a shrink!

We began by formally welcoming everyone and once more introducing ourselves to the rest of the team. There were some discussions regarding ongoing project updates before splitting into groups for separate workshops. Throughout the course of the afternoon, we had individual chats with Clive (in the presence of Wil) to check on progress, well-being, personal goals, developments etc.

Not only was the afternoon game of touch rugby on the beach becoming familiar in the team build calendar, the 0600 hours "generator start up", was continued from the days of the very first training sails, followed by a P.T. session. By the end of the weekend, a concerned furrow began to periodically cast a shadow over Clive's brow as he counted the injury numbers, slowly climbing.

After breakfast on Saturday morning a little more was explained to us about one of the features of the weekend. After a short drive in the VW People-Carrier that we had been lent, it became apparent what this particular exercise was to be. We drove through the gates of H.M.S. Excellent and were directed towards the car park for DRIU. Damage Repair Instruction Unit.

DRIU has just celebrated her tenth birthday. In 1994 she was a £12 million simulated Type 23 Frigate structure, who's job was to simulate, using hydraulic rams etc. the motions and environment of a vessel holed whilst under attack at sea. The huge reservoir of water chilled to 8 degrees, which stands right next to her, looked ominous.

The reasons why we had spent nearly three hours in health and safety briefings, briefings on mending holes in metal plate the size of a football, with water ejecting at 120 psi, being dressed in thermals and waterproof clothing and finally, being given a hammer each, were becoming obvious.

Later, after de-brief, Sue also accepted the task of teaching 7eam to dance.

In the video footage, there is a scene reminiscent of an extract from Mary Shelley's "Doctor Frankenstein" where, with his head in his hands, Doctor Frankenstein cries in despair "My God! I have created a monster!"

Sunday brought more P.T. followed by reviews of goals and values and an update on tasks completed, outstanding and in development. The greater part of the day was spent with Wil and the subject of Focus.

11

Nicko, the cool kid, rolling up on his scooter!

Talk about making an appearance.

He rolled into town with his computer under his arm, turned on the charm and became a firm favourite with everyone from that moment onwards.

Sure, your blood's worth bottling Nicko.

The others brought our introduction to outside assistance.

I had expected a weather and routing expert and the fitness and diet were quite a welcome discipline for me. It turned out that my diet and regime were quite good.

I bought into that stuff okay.

What I wasn't really expecting was the psychoanalyst. Wil describes himself as a stretch and not a shrink. That's a fair description I suppose it's just that I didn't realise that we needed one.

We did.

These guys continued working with the team and were a significant help to the project, working with Clive in particular right up until the end of the race.

Sue reported the story of DRIU (Damage Repair Instruction Unit – A sinking ship simulator to you and me) on the team website a few weeks later. The simulator there resembles a sinking warship. You're inside the hull, the Captain announces an imminent air-strike over the tannoy and there is a loud bang, the boat shudders and the lights go out. Loads of freezing water comes pouring out of various size holes and the place starts filling up with water and smoke, then the emergency lighting comes on and you begin lurching around like a disabled ship really. You have to plug the holes before you sink.

A bit like the fairground game where you hit heads with a hammer as they randomly pop up from underneath trap doors.

Colder though….. and wetter……obviously.

TB3 took place a couple of weeks later; my summary for the 7eam website was as follows;

For the weekend of 26 – 28th March, Clive had organised TB3. The Charter of a couple of Sunfast 37's from Sunsail U.K., a yacht charter company based at Port Solent, a well established commercial sailing centre, near Portsmouth.

Sunsail regularly host weekend regattas using their fleet of 37-foot long yachts, and this weekend 7eam had chartered two of them, with a view to taking part in the fun.

With twenty-one yachts entered, the promise was of a reasonable size fleet, although the weather forecast was at odds with the synoptic charts and although the forecast was for wind strengths between force 3 and 4, it was hard to believe.

Most of us met up on Friday evening and had a meal and liquid refreshments at the excellent facilities offered in Port Solent. We split into two groups and slept on our allocated yachts, numbers 60 and 63.

When Clive arrived early on Saturday morning, instead of finding us still asleep, hungover, or worse still, not yet arrived, he found laptop computers, yacht racing rule books, tidal charts and weather forecasts all being pored over by an enthusiastic bunch of people, keen as anything to get on the water.

So far so good.

The skippers briefing took place at 0830 hours and by just after 0900 hours, we slipped dock, went through the lock and made our way towards Gilkicker Point, off Gosport in the Solent, to the race area.

In the absence of any wind to mention, the race committee delayed the start for an hour.

By 1120 hours there was enough wind to race. A course was set and a warning signal made to inform us that it was ten minutes to race start.

The fleet had a clean start and all boats were away. The first incident then occurred. Various calls and exchanges were made as yacht 63, sandwiched between two other yachts (who shall remain numberless), careered towards the first mark at 3 knots! As the first buoy came into view, they all tried to fit into the space the size of one yacht.

One of the basic rules in yacht racing, rule 14, is to avoid contact and the onus is on all competitors to abide by that rule, regardless of rights of way, to avoid damage.

A protest was later lodged against yacht 63.

The results of the first race yacht 60 – 11th place, yacht 63 – 8th place.

The afternoon race brought no major incidents and to our surprise, once again, yachts 60 and 63 finished within a couple of places for the second time that day. The results, yacht 60 – 7th place, yacht 63 – 5th place.

On Saturday evening, we moored in Gun Wharf Quay, which is the mooring venue for the Challenge fleet in September, prior to Race start. The skyline is dominated by Spinnaker Tower, an abstract design depicting a mast and spinnaker towering above the marina.

Due to his sky-diving experience, Phil's first thought was, "Could I jump off that?"

Aside from that, there are shops, restaurants and bars, all housed in a new development which offers pretty much all you would want if you were in the final stages of preparation for a global yacht race. Handy that.

Sunday, Day Two, brought light winds once again and further task rotations aboard so that we all had opportunity to complete a variety of tasks.

The clocks had been adjusted to British Summer Time overnight and as we waited for the warning signal, one competitor was heard to radio the committee boat to inform them that they would be late for the start.

Both yachts from 7eam had changed their clocks. This time on race one, it was yacht 60's turn to mis-judge and Rich managed to hit the first mark. After completing a 360 degree turn to exonerate themselves for the mistake, they found themselves near the back of the fleet. Slowly they worked their way back up the fleet and once again managed to finish within a couple of places of their team mates. Yacht 60 – 12th place, yacht 63 – 9th place.

Race four on Sunday afternoon brought the classic point of the whole regatta. Not only had we had a protest lodged and a mark rounding badly mis-judged, we finished the weekend with a collision (very minor) between yachts 60 and 63! Yacht 60 – 11th place, yacht 63 – 8th place.

We were constantly being reminded over the entire weekend that we were there to continue our team building efforts, being reinforced with briefings and de-briefings, however, tell twenty helmsmen to all go to the same place, at the same time, after saying "On your marks, Get set, Go!" and, well, what do you expect?

The overall positions put yacht 60 in 10th place and yacht 63 in 8th place.

Phil won the Team Seven Trophy for driving Yacht 60 when it hit Yacht 63, he was vilified for no good reason though as there were plenty of other incidents within the team which could have justified receiving the award.

Ruth took an interesting photo of me polishing a scuff mark out of the hull before we got back in.

It didn't appear on the website.

The Challenge yachts were getting some attention too.

£3.8 m worth.

For the first time in the race's history, the re-fit in preparation for the race was almost completely managed by Challenge Business in-house.

The exception was the paint work on the hull and top deck which was undertaken by Berthon in their impressive facilities at Lymington.

The hulls were stripped of all but essential fittings and two at a time, they were motored up to Berthon's Yard.

Once there, the hulls were stripped of the remaining fittings, sandblasted, sprayed with an epoxy primer and their first coat of anti-fouling applied.

They were then moved into a preparation booth and the three coats of paint necessary for each hull are applied in one day and kept in a constant environment at thirty degrees Celsius, allowing the paint to cure overnight. They could then be moved outside for the first coat of non-slip deck paint, the essential deck fittings replaced and motored back down to Plymouth for the rest of the work to continue.

I could see their masts from my front room window.

When I went sailing after work, they were there.

When I peered out of the bedroom window at night, I could hear the rattle of the halyards pinging inside the masts, as the wind rocked the cradle.

I often cycled out of my way by about four miles on my way home from work at night to stop and look at them in their various states of preparation or undress.

Photos appeared on the website.

The rudders were dropped out of the hull and the cables, needle bearings, pedestal and controls were removed and replaced. The pulpits and pushpits were re-polished or replaced, a new Harken winch set fitted, all the wiring completely checked and/or replaced.

They had new masts and rigging, new sails, new cookers and ovens, the water-makers, generators, SSB and VHF radios and all the B&G instruments were returned to their manufacturers for service and re-warranty.

It was exhaustive and slowly they started appearing on the hard standing at Plymouth Yacht Haven.

On the week beginning April 19th, the crews started arriving in Plymouth. Not all crew were required to attend but Team Seven managed an almost complete turn out.

Things started moving along.

The sails arrived and the resulting human caterpillars trundled down the pontoons as the mainsails were fitted.

For the next week there was non-stop activity as cars, vans and lorries formed an almost constant flow of arrivals and departures of fixtures and fittings, which were added to or taken away from the fleet and fixed, measured and adjusted to our soon-to-be homes.

By extreme co-incidence, on April 21st when Sony fitted the new computers, yacht #43 had another permanent fixture, which we kept until the end of the race.

Another permanent fixture, which was the team computer, in a manner of speaking was Nicko, who moved into bunk number 14, he also brought his laptop, scooter and his Didgeridoo.

Phil brought a *Minky* ironing board and a small iron in preparation for some *Extreme Ironing* and Kate later brought an inflatable globe which was an extremely useful prop.

All of these items fell outside of the personal luxury item(s) with a mandatory one kilo weight limit, which we would be allowed to take with us.

There were to be some special exceptions.

The work was finished on time and to budget.

When the refit was officially completed the yachts were 'handed over' to their respective teams at Plymouth Yacht Haven on Thursday 29th April.

The press were there, as were some family and friends. The Challenge technical team were also there, which was a good job as they were still working on the boats.

That morning, the fleet motored out of the Cattewater, past my flat in Sutton

Harbour and into the waters of Plymouth Sound. We made a parade across the foreshore, beneath the Citadel and the Hoe, out towards Firestone Bay and Drake's Island.

We cleared Plymouth Breakwater at the Eastern Entrance passed the Great Mewstone Rock and Yealm Head and got sailing for the first time together. As the short chop of the English Channel and the North Easterly winds started bashing into us, some of the crew started feeling distinctly green. The wind speed rose to twenty-five knots as we cleared Bolt Head.

Phil, Mike and I went up on the bow to change down from the Number One Yankee.

I should've known it. I should have held back. I should've offered to do the sheet. I was going to be a bowman and it was entirely my own fault for volunteering.

Fool!

I didn't really want to work the bow, it wouldn't have been my first choice but I knew that I would be useful up there, so, if thinking 'Best for Boat' I knew where my place was.

It gets pretty bouncy up there sometimes and I'd done *Number Two Bow* on the Challenge Business Round Britain & Ireland Race a year previously. I knew why bowmen were revered in certain circles, it was because it was a dangerous place to work and the people that worked there seemed oblivious to that fact.

As well as being great logical thinkers, they have super-human strength.

They sneer in the face of danger and they leap in where Angels fear to tread.

They have no apparent concept of personal safety.

They are absolutely nuts.

Phil would be good as a bowman

I was resigned to my fate, but I didn't sneer, leap, had a deeply held concept of self-preservation and arguably, wasn't nuts.

The good news was that Phil was to be my *Number One Bowman*. He was someone I knew I could work with. O.K. so he had brought the ironing board, but that wasn't what it seemed and he was a big strong guy, practical beyond most people's grasp, fearless, an electrician, all round mechanic, listened to punk music, died his hair and had an opinion on every subject that you could raise.

When you didn't raise one, he did.

He also brought along a copy of the Profanasaurus.

Phil introduced himself to the Challenge staff as a qualified *'Sparks'* and was able to get his teeth into the wiring and mechanics on board.

He helped us out time and time again and was a fundamental team member.

When we discovered an alarming amount of water in the bilges on

Thursday afternoon during the delivery and training sail up to Saint Kat's we quickly realised that there were still going to be some teething problems from the re-fit to be sorted out.

The water outlet hadn't been connected properly to the hull and it was leaking.

It took some time to discover where the water was coming from, but when we did, Phil and Paul fixed it.

Another fault appeared, common to the whole fleet.

This time it was with the sail build which we discovered when one of the mainsails ripped during a reef. The fittings weren't aligned properly and the resulting, uneven pressure when the reef was put in caused the mainsail to rip.

They all had to go back to Hood's sail loft for adjustment.

A number of minor problems materialized, but the resulting crew/boat familiarization process was an invaluable time and we learnt many things that would come in useful later in the race.

Some of the crews begrudged these jobs, thinking that the Challenge staff should have done more as a part of the refit. I felt that it was a great time to get to know each other and our boat thoroughly; the Challenge staff were never far away and were as helpful as they could possibly have been.

We covered every inch of that boat between then and the race start. Meanwhile, we plodded on with the St. Kat's delivery.

Sea-sickness was becoming rife, we weren't used to living together, we kept getting in each others way and the boat leaked.

It wasn't slick.

Robin Price, a reporter with the Western Morning News newspaper, sailed up with us and wrote about his journey a couple of weeks later in the paper.

It was entitled *'From the sick, to the slick'*.

It got us some attention.

On Friday night we stopped off at Ramsgate Marina and picked up *Flash* (Tim Johnston) who was still under-cover as he hadn't told his employers of his plans to take part in the race and hadn't been able to get the day off work without drawing suspicion, so he appeared under cover of darkness.

Alex's parents had collected Flash from the train station, as they lived locally, and had dropped him to the marina. They stayed around to say hello and slipped Alex some chocolate bars.

I saw them Alex.

If you're going to eat in class, you have to share!

By the time we had reached Dover, the wind dropped away to virtually nothing and the fog rolled in. We dropped and packed the headsails and motor-sailed up the Thames together as a fleet. We were all shouting and *Three Cheering!* anything we could think of that morning as we made our way up the Thames from just before dawn.

We thought we were cheering at the people watching us from their windows and balconies at that time in the morning.

The people watching us from their windows and balconies probably would have said they were looking to find out what all the noise was about at that time in the morning, had they been asked.

Nobody asked them.

We cheered louder, more came out.

'Three cheers for Team Seven'

Look at us!

Between 9.15 – 10.15am on Saturday 1st May, the fleet made a parade of sail underneath Tower Bridge in London and we then moored up in Saint Katharine's Dock for a weekend of fun.

As we passed through the lock-gate and were waiting for the water levels to equalize, we nipped below deck and changed into our Team Seven shore clothing.

We had busted a gut to get all the shirts, jackets and trousers all the right size, embroidered and delivered on time so that we could fulfill the Challenge recommendation to the skippers that we should appear as a professional, organised set up.

We passed the test with flying colours.

On Saturday we opened the boats up for friends and family to visit.

Sunday was designated as a Public Open Day and the official naming ceremony of the Barclays Adventurer.

The long weekend, with a Bank Holiday Monday, was also a good opportunity for us to flog some merchandise to pay some of the bills that had been accumulating.

You're in the spotlight ... Kate Stainsby.

Kate had taken up the role of merchandising. Despite having no expertise in that area, she dived in head first and bamboozled everyone.

She had spent hours and hours on the phone or e-mailing suppliers and manufacturers, in a non-stop barrage of pleading and fact finding. Everything from shore clothing and technical clothing to sleeping bags, T-shirts and mugs, shoes, trainers, loads!

She also helped out with writing reports for the team website occasionally.

She was another crew member that I instantly liked.

I hadn't yet met anybody that I actively dis-liked, but I am not the sort of person that instantly likes everybody that I meet, so it's unusual for me to like someone straight away.

We (Kate) had ordered a load of T-shirts and drinking mugs with our new logo on to sell.

This was our first opportunity to actually raise some money to pay some of our accumulating bills.

We had also come up with the idea of putting the crew members up for Adoption. Give us £50 and we will give you a new friend, bearing gifts of a mug and a T-shirt they would also send postcards from the stop-over ports. Small scale stuff really, but it was a start and we needed it.

The weekend was a great success. We changed into our 7eam shore clothing and set up a stall on the Dockside.

The sun shone and the people came.

We took over £1,200.00 that weekend,

Kate was off the hook.

A couple of funny things happened that weekend.

Firstly;

After being shown around the boat in the afternoon and meeting some of the crew members, we were adopted by two Australian visitors named Angel and Robert. They donated £1,000 to our team fund.

Nobody had expected that to happen.

The difficulty we had was that we didn't have a thousand pounds worth of anything to give them in return.

Secondly;

Whilst we were actually in the lock on our way into Saint Kat's Dock, getting changed and throwing mooring lines around, a few people had called over to us from the quayside and occasionally someone would catch your eye and ask about the trip up or something similar. One person asked me a question and I answered it, but somehow she was engaging me more than other people were.

She seemed *really* interested in our boat and kept asking me questions.

It was no surprise then when, during the open day, the same girl came over to us and asked if she could possibly have a look aboard. It turned out that she had just followed a whim and put her name down as reserve crew for the race and may be taking part in some or all of it. She had come to us because we were *'the friendliest'* crew.

Her name was Paula Jane Reid.

She couldn't sail and I don't think she bought one of Kate's T-shirts or mugs.

The team building sessions took a back seat during the early part of late

May and early June, as the next session for some was the Round Britain & Ireland Race.

Eight of the fleet took part and it took place between Sunday 30th May and Friday 11th June.

As well as Clive having a mate, Quentin Dimmer, taking part in this race, Nicko, Newton, Alex and Mike were aboard 7eam taking advantage of an offer that Challenge Business put out, which enabled each boat to have a maximum of four of their 'Global Core Crew' take part alongside the Round Britain Crew.

7eam were oversubscribed, Sue raced with Matt Riddell on *Besso Racing*.

I couldn't get the time off work, besides I crewed on it the previous year, as a part of my own training regime.

So did Clive.

The *RBI* as its known, started on Sunday 30th May and Team Seven got off the line first. They hoisted their kites and headed down towards Land's End and Waypoint Alpha.

The whole fleet made great speed and Team Seven hit the waypoint, just ahead of BP Explorer and Kunachi, in first place.

Those that couldn't sail, watched the whole thing from the Challenge website.

Day and night.

A couple of days later Clive wrote a report from aboard, which was posted on the official race website.

"Two days ago we rounded Waypoint Alpha at the front of the fleet, kite up and heading north! Since then it has been a drag race pushed along by a strong westerly flow.

BP over took the other night when we took our kite down.

Since then we have been chasing. However, they are still within sight. If we had kept our kite up, maybe we would still be in front. But then possibly we could have blown it and with more than half the race still to run, we have to be conservative with the sail."

There were sails being tested in various conditions and they studied boat speed versus sail plan.

There was some fun as they sailed up towards the Irish Sea and got buzzed by an R.A.F. Nimrod who contacted them by V.H.F. radio to inform them that they were entering a live surface to air missile testing area.

His best advice was that we *get the hell out of there*! (My words, not his.)

There were some frantic telephone and radio calls from the race yachts back to Challenge Race Office and them and the Royal Navy, eventually the matter was sorted and the fleet was allowed to carry on racing.

Team Seven were first around Muckle Flugga (A little village right on the Northern tip of the Shetland Isles.) the imaginary half way point where you turn around and start going south.

It was a psychological boost.

Clive wrote another report a couple of days later;

"Rounded Muckle Flugga at 1325 BST, BP approx 4nm behind, managed to get past under a 20kt squall and by hugging the coast for more breeze and of course trim trim trim - there is always more boat speed to be had. Beautiful place not like 12 months ago when it was blowing 30kts on the nose and S of S (Spirit of Southampton) had stolen a forty mile lead on us. 12kts over the ground tide helping us towards Smith Knoll - still plenty more racing before the squadron line with a high moving in for another tactical battle, in such conditions races are won and lost! Seven days ago exactly we led down the Solent now we are leading the way at the other end of the course after a battle all the way up the west coast."

Clive Cosby

After rounding Muckle Flugga, Kunachi (who were third place at the time) gambled by going slightly further east than BP Explorer and Team Seven and it paid.

They took the lead.

The struggle for positions continued down the North Sea though and BP and Team Seven kept up the pressure on them all the way to the line. BP Explorer got through them twenty-four hours before race finish to take the line honours.

Team Seven finished in third place on Friday 11th June just after 1420 hours and some of us went up to Southampton after work to help them party.

They just wanted to read newspapers.

Challenge Business Round Britain & Ireland Race 2004
Overall Positions

BP Explorer
Kunachi
Team Seven
Barclays Adventurer
SAIC
The Firm
Team Save the Children

Besso Racing

A great exercise and some valuable experience gained, with a good result thrown in.

For Clive and Nicko it was a valuable time, recording data of all kinds that could affect boat speed, including sail combinations in various wind strengths, boat speed and wind speed compared to the apparent wind angle etc. They discussed when to change sails and when not to, when to push a little bit harder and when to be satisfied with performance levels, the instruments were getting calibrated and things were coming together.

They were all able to test the food that was to be our diet and learn little anomalies about preparation.

Mike was lined up as a potential watch leader, so was Alex.

Newton and Sue got some experience sailing offshore.

It was a great success.

Team Seven grew in confidence.

It started getting silly, some of the crew started putting heroic signatures on their e-mails, then came the time to choose a boat theme song or tune to establish our identity when we left or entered a port during the race start or finish.

What should have happened, was that Clive should have chosen one

We all got to nominate one and second vote another.

Some of the nominated songs were bordering on the absurd and some were okay.

Most were not.

We went down the route of having democratic elections with Proportionate Representation. Eventually all the proposals and secondary votes were cast and the song that won was deemed not suitable by Clive.

We had a re-vote and the same song won with a slight swing in electorate loyalties.

It wasn't a rude song or anything, just maybe not serious enough and we wanted to be taken seriously.

Clive chose the song.

'Praise You' by Fatboy Slim.

The Qualifying sail (Friday July 2nd – Sunday July 11th) was the last official training sail and was compulsory for all current crew to attend.

It was a ten day sailing programme, during which a whole manner of systems and roles were put into place and tested.

Challenge orchestrated the whole thing, but we also made up our own scenarios and as a team, prepared ourselves further.

It was also a time for Clive to assess individuals' capabilities in order for him to designate roles and responsibilities; it was also another chance for us to further familiarize ourselves with our boat and to make it our own.

As I had been writing the reports for the website and taking all the photos from the time of the crew selection, mine was the role of *Media* amongst other things.

The following is my first on-board log submitted to Challenge Race Office.

Daily Report Friday 2nd July 2004 (My birthday!)

Friday 2nd of July saw team seven assemble at Ocean Village in preparation for the Global Challenge 2004/5 Qualifying Sail.

Team Seven crewmembers were organised to visit the Quays Leisure Centre in Southampton over the next two days to be the subject of further vigorous fitness tests, courtesy of Vale Sesto.
Of equal importance was the fact that I was celebrating my 38th birthday, the evening started well with me passing the fitness test, it then progressed nicely to a meal aboard the yacht before degenerating to an evening with the crew at the infamous Frog & Frigate. The bruise on my noggin shows no signs of receding!

On Saturday morning, all the crews of the challenge fleet attended a briefing on what we could expect in the coming nine days. Needless to say Challenge Business have some surprises up their sleeves for us by way of emergency scenarios and general race preparation. Each yacht also sent two crewmembers to a presentation on behalf of Sony, who supply the computers and both digital still and video cameras. Unfortunately, we are still in the development stages and cannot send the edited video films and still masterpieces at present, more later.

During the course of the day many more jobs were tackled and completed and a few more were added to the list. A huge job is the food preparation and packaging, ably performed by Ruth, Kate& Sarah.

We made our way to the dominant skyline feature of Spinnaker Tower on GunWharf Quay on Saturday afternoon, with a view to mooring there for the night before the start on Sunday afternoon.

Unfortunately, as we came alongside the quay, beam on to 30 knots of breeze, one of the mooring lines snagged Ruth's right leg and for a moment she was tangled up. The result was a badly bruised leg and the skin taken off her knuckles and whilst this was fairly shocking for everyone at the time, I'm pleased to report that she was not too badly hurt. (I shy away from saying she was lucky!)

She, Kate and Clive, after a trip to the local hospital were able to join us for food later on, even though we'd finished.

The whole crew were up at 0630 hours on Sunday morning and out on the water for the two practice starts at 1030hrs and 1130hrs respectively and the start proper for 1250hrs. After some cracking starts we were off down the Solent with one crewmember broken toed, one skinless knuckled and one with a swollen noggin!
Keep watching!

Richard Parson
Team Stelmar

The injury list was apparently showing no signs of let up. A lesson that we were still to learn was that we should take care of things and don't break them, especially people.

Still no sponsor, but we could flog you a mug, a t-shirt, a ticket to come aboard the Ocean Scene to watch the race start or you could 'Adopt' one of the crew members and get a goody bag, postcards and e-mails from stop-overs etc.. We were getting logs and photos that we sent from the boat, onto our 7eam website daily.

We began to attract the interest of some of the other teams and there were whispers that '7eam' were well organized.

We actually began to get registered supporters, proper ones.

We were getting 5,000 hits a month on the team website at this time.

The reports were getting a little long winded I admit.

Challenge business organised a seminar with various media bods, they recommended that we keep our reports down to between 200-250 words.

I took heed, although I was becoming pretty adept with typing using the computer keyboard. I know that doesn't sound difficult, but the roll and pitch of the boat meant that it was far from easy, as it and you were thrown around in all directions. I bought some double sided Velcro and taped the keyboard and the camera battery charger to the little ledge at the back of the boat which meant that it didn't keep sliding around, or fall off the ledge and get broken.

We all started making little adjustments to the boat and our gear to make our lives easier.

From crockery racks, to communal *shower bags* to contain our shared toothpastes, shampoo, shaving kit and all the bathroom accessories that we wanted, to little drying lines to hang our kit from when we were trying to dry it out. Photos started appearing above our bunks, press clippings were pasted to the galley walls.

We began to take ownership of the boat.

<u>Daily Report Tuesday 6th July</u>

Today brought more of the same light winds that we experienced overnight on Monday.

In many ways light winds require more concentration than the heavy stuff, especially when the sun is beating down as it saps the energy just as surely as the most vigorous of exercise does. Sun cream, hats and plenty of water are necessary to keep the mind focused, as is the constant pinging of the wrist-watch alarm that is attached to the aluminium frame that surrounds the wheel.

The alarm springs to life at regular intervals to remind us to record data, regularly we altar positions on the boat to keep fresh. The crew member next in line to take the helm sitting with the current helm to monitor progress and prepare for their turn, the crew members trimming the spinnaker swap around from winching to trimming etc.

The day has shown a good run despite the lack of wind and for the best part of the day our competitors have been within sight of us.

Shortly before watch change over this evening at 2000 hours there was another medical emergency. Most of the crew were on deck when Doctor Ruth (herself an earlier casualty) called out from the foredeck that she needed some help as "Flash" had received a blow to the head.

Assistance was rendered immediately in an ordered manner as some of the crew made their way forward leaving the helm and two crewmembers to keep sailing the boat.
"Flash" was conscious, although obviously in some discomfort and lying on the deck.

However, all was not as it seemed! On closer inspection, the first diagnosis was that the blow must have come from a tomato sauce bottle, presumably from Doctor Ruth herself!

The medical "emergency" was quickly and effectively dealt with as a neck brace was fitted to our casualty and a bunk was dismantled for use as a tem-

porary stretcher as "Flash" was taken below decks for a more thorough examination and medical treatment.

I am pleased to report that by the time we had a de-briefing, twenty minutes later, Doctor Ruth had worked her magic and Flash was once again, fighting fit.

Richard Parson
Team Stelmar

Our awkwardness moving around the boat was a real handicap.

I was helming and for some reason Newton was standing at the back of the boat.

When the boat rolled, Newton lost his balance and fell.

I caught him.

My leg was outstretched so that I could balance and he landed on my knee, forcing it inwards.

It was lucky for him because he had his fall broken and was unhurt.

I suffered a strained ligament and tendon.

For a moment, everything stopped.

There was no light, no sounds and nothing around me.

My whole body, everything that I normally felt, sensed and was aware of, moved to my head.

My mind opened its eye and although I couldn't physically see anything, I was totally focused on one thing only.

My knee.

I could hardly stand it.

Kate strapped it up and I rested it for a while.

When we got back ashore, I spent time and money on a sports physiotherapist who, with the aid of an ultra-sound device and plenty of manipulation, fixed me up.

From that moment on, whenever anyone was near me, I expected them to fall on me.

A couple of times they did, but as I was braced to accept them, they always bounced off me and it hurt them not me.

Daily Report 8th July

As dawn broke on Thursday 8th July, the wind was steadily blowing at twenty knots.

As it had been building for the past twenty-four hours the sea state was also increasing and the waves were now considerably higher than the one metre swell of yesterday.

We rounded the Fastnet Rock overnight and were now making our way to the next waypoint "Western Approaches", barreling along at a maximum boat speed of nearly sixteen knots in winds gusting up to thirty knots.

For some of the crew, this was the fastest that they had ever travelled on board a Challenge yacht and for all of us, the feeling was pitched somewhere between complete exhilaration and nervous tension.

The morning watch had already succeeded in blowing apart the one and a half ounce promo kite (our biggest spinnaker) and we were now in a quandary as to whether to drop our only other spinnaker before blowing that one apart as well and therefore reduce our boat speed or stick with it and gain every possible advantage that we could.

As there were other yachts on the horizon, we decided to stay with the spinnaker, although on more than a couple of occasions we adopted the positions to retrieve it and change down to something more manageable, each time deciding to stick with it a little longer.

Down below the mother watch continued the daily chores of cleaning the boat and preparing the food and hot and cold drinks for those "up top". Although the action is all going on on deck, below deck there are a hundred and one other activities that are going on to keep the yacht working efficiently, driving in the right direction and making sure the crews can race and push the boat, twenty four hours a day.

Right now, I'm of to sleep after six hours on mother watch, to make sure that I am fit to do it all again when I get a wake up shout in a few hours time.

We broached the boat on the way back to Southampton.

We were sailing by the lee to try and round a mark when we went into an involuntary gybe. (Basically, we were sailing at a perilous angle to the wind direction. The wind caught the wrong side of the mainsail and made it swing uncontrollably across the boat, resulting in the boat lying flat in the water.)

The ensuing mayhem was clearly visible to most of the other boats.

We had lost control of the boat.

It was embarrassing.

I had been helming most of the day and being a downwind course, thought that I was sailing to one of my strong points.

It became evident to me that we weren't going to be able to sail so low that we could round a mark of the course without gybing.

I told Clive, he grabbed the wheel.

I felt that we would have to gybe at some point.

Clive disagreed, he drove, we gybed involuntarily and some of us went swimming.

It took the wind out of our sails.

Following the qualifying sail, Sarah Lamb had some bad news for us. She officially resigned from the crew on 14th July.

Her father was due to take part in the race aboard Sony Viao but was having personal difficulties with Amadeo Sorrentino the skipper.

Sarah was a student. She had little enough money to cover her berth fee. Her father had reportedly agreed to give her half of any money that he raised through sponsorship to help her and he had raised a large amount for himself and therefore was able to greatly ease the financial burden for her.

When he decided to pull out, he also withdrew his offer to her.

Inevitably, Sarah was no longer in a position to pay for her space. She had been in the final year of her degree course and was reluctant to get totally committed to the team builds and other activities until after her exams.

Besides which, her father was investing in a new boat and her boyfriend was planning to travel to Bermuda to work on charter yachts and she wanted to go with him.

I found it hard to understand.

Maybe she loved the guy?

I don't know.

Within a week Clive was phoning us all to pass on the news that we had a new crew-member to replace Sarah.

Her name was Paula Jane Reid.

She was a different kettle of fish.

Paula had been interviewed by Challenge in March and had been put on the waiting list.

She was the girl that we had met in Saint Katharine's Dock.

On Monday 19th July she received a call from Challenge Business to say she was going to take part in the race with 7eam. Reportedly, she was sitting on the toilet at work when the phone rang.

Just as well I heard.

That evening, on the telephone conference call, she was introduced to the team. By Friday 23rd July, she had driven down to the boat and was ready to go sailing with us on a race training sail.

The sailing was from Friday 24th July to Thursday 29th. We had arrived on Friday evening and Vale had selected some of us to attend a personal fitness and strength assessment at a local gym, whilst fitted with a heart rate monitor. She measured our body mass and checked our progress on the fitness programmes that she had written for us.

With the exception of Mike, who wasn't playing at all, we were given the opportunity to study our fitness levels and do something about them, if we wanted to.

I did.

I passed the test.

The following day was Clive's birthday.

Phil had begun to establish himself within the team by now and many conversations had already taken an in depth look at the benefits of his wicking underpants. Subsequently, Clive was presented with a new pair for his birthday which he promptly modelled for us.

Paula, our new princess, wondered what on earth was happening.

"Clive's birthday was on the 24th - the day we set off, he was given those wicking pants and he posed around in them and I wondered what on earth my skipper was like! I was extremely nervous and didn't know anyone or anything. I was sick. And I had to clear up that awful breakfast Sue had managed to spread and burn all over the galley - porridge and scrambled egg everywhere! Burnt egg made everyone feel sick. I think I won my brownie points then....."

Paula Reid

The sickness passed and the wind dropped away.

We spent a lot of time drifting around.

At one stage, we spent a few hours motoring in reverse so that we could generate enough apparent wind to fill the lightest spinnaker and practice gybing it. There was enough to do though, we busied ourselves with countless number of jobs and were never idle.

It was a productive time.

During August, there were some corporate responsibilities involving a day or two at a time, sailing around the Solent with business guests and yacht sponsors. We packed beautifully prepared, fresh food, beer, wine, fruit juices etc. which we served for lunch and generally had a relaxing, pleasant day.

They were interesting days generally and gave us a chance to talk to people about what we were doing, now that we were beginning to understand ourselves.

I officially left work on Thursday 2nd September, collected a hire van with my Dad and drove from Plymouth to Clive's rented house in Southampton to collect a whole load of cardboard boxes. The weekend of 4 & 5th September was scheduled as the *Food Pack Weekend,*

I was obligated to a sail training weekend as it would appear that I had somehow missed my *Consolidation Sail* (one of the scheduled training courses) and therefore would have to go sailing during the day and helping to pack the food during the night.

As if that wasn't bad enough. There was also a BBC Television reporter coming to interview me about the race on Saturday and a Media course on Monday.

I was annoyed at myself for having missed a scheduled part of the training, but I was also annoyed at the timing of the weekend and naturally, Challenge insisted that I take part. I had messed up a little, this time it was my fault. I had simply missed a part of the training programme.

Dad drove the hired van back to Plymouth after we had emptied it of all the contents of Clive's garage and got home late after a very long day.

I stepped aboard one of the Challenge 67's (the 67 feet boats that had been used in the '92 and '96 races and were currently used for training purposes) at about 10.00pm.

Paula was on the same sail.

She was working her socks off with training sails and she had been as busy as any of us. She was almost sailing full time to soak up as much information as possible as well as organize her working life and her home life. With a never ending supply of wet sailing gear to wash and dry somehow before going out to sea again and then staying up all night for a few days.

You get the idea?

Although she will admit, she came to us with very little sailing knowledge; there was no doubt about her enthusiasm and dedication to the project, demonstrated when we were looking for a model to have their photograph taken to send to one of our food suppliers.

In order to demonstrate that their foods were ideal for preparing and eating in the harshest conditions, they had asked us to supply a photo for publicity use.

The trouble was, there was not a breath of wind.

Hardly harsh.

Paula got her foul weather gear on, crouched in the cockpit with a bag of food and a fork and smiled as four of us armed with buckets of water and one of us (me) with a camera, surrounded her.

At the count of three ....

Great photos!

Ruth was next to feel the spotlight.

She was responsible, together with Vale, for the food and diet, as well as ordering and overseeing the whole pack. We had an Asda articulated lorry deliver our food and provisions on Friday 3rd September and we moved it into the marquee that Challenge have, on the quay at Ocean Village.

The job was a huge one.

We worked 24 hours a day for the whole weekend, I pretty much forgot all about the training sail after the first couple of days (Thanks Quiggles!) and worked flat out with the others to separate, pack and vacuum seal all the provisions that we were getting shipped to the various stop-over ports in the world to feed us for the coming legs.

The only interruption to the schedule came on Saturday evening when Clive and Vale had organized a *Friends and Family* barbeque.

The evening basically had one message.

We had a sponsor.

Stelmar Shipping Limited were to be our main yacht sponsor.

Stelmar was based in Greece but with offices in London and were an oil shipping brokerage.

Perfect.

They would know all about the sea and shipping.

We could have been a Teddy Bear boat. (I know, they liked it! I know!)

We had relevance!

Team Stelmar eh?

Sounds alright.

Now what do we do?

It was a long tiring weekend and on Monday afternoon, Mike, Nicko and I drove the food down to the Challenge Offices at the Plymouth Watersports Centre and unloaded it onto pallets before going home and falling asleep on the sofa.

The following weekend, a few of us went to Mike's house in Dorset to finish off the job properly.

We did a good job.

The team website was re-named and by now, www.teamstelmar.com was getting about 9,000 hits a month.

I felt it was important to keep the news and reports coming and had basically taken over that side of things in the absence of any other volunteers. I also set myself up as *Official Photographer*, making sure that I recorded our progress and gave our supporters something to look at and read.

Kate, Phil, Julian and Sue all contributed and of course Nicko created it, but he had let me do my own thing pretty much since the RBI race in May/June and I was working on that as one of my jobs within the team.

Instead of getting up in the mornings and smoking a cigarette with my cup of tea, I logged on and employed the time more usefully.

I spent a week at home with my fiancée, at the beginning of September and we tried to spend some time dedicated to each other. I couldn't settle and we didn't really talk to one another, we just put our heads down and went on as though nothing was happening.

On Monday 20th September I left my flat and officially moved aboard. The fleet were in Gunwharf Quays now and there were still many jobs that needed completing so I went a week earlier than we were expected, as did a few of the others and we continued progress on the jobs list.

We were effectively invading Nicko's home and for the first time since April 21st he moved out, to the Holiday Inn Express on Gunwharf Quay.

On Friday 24th all crew were to be aboard. We ate together in the evening; it was a poignant moment for many.

We had slept at home for the last time, pulled the door closed into the frame behind us and handed the keys over to someone else.

We had left home.

There were some tears.

Tina came up to Portsmouth on Saturday 25th September and we spent the final week together staying in a B&B on Spice Island, choosing not to stay with the rest of the crew in the organised team accommodation.

Our rooms took the top floor of a B&B, a great view and a little balcony with a table and chairs.

Perfect.

For me.

During the day there was work to do on the boat, R.O.R.C. inspections, Challenge Business courses, Safety briefings, schools visits and meetings, most of the evenings we either worked on late or had some official function that we were to attend. I was in two teams at this point and I didn't really do justice to either.

Tina and I had a couple of nights together, tucked up in our B&B, laying on the bed, drinking wine and watching the ferries and yachts sailing right past the open French doors.

I dreamed of adventures at sea.

She thought it was cold.

Leg One – Portsmouth to Buenos Aires.

(Leggers – Adrian Stafford-Jones, Tony Rogers)

On the morning of the race I was up early and ate breakfast with my family and friends that had stayed overnight at the same B&B.

I went down to meet the crew at Loch Fyne restaurant at 0730 hours, ate another breakfast and was told to meet back at the boat in an hour.

I went back to the B&B and had another coffee.

Nobody had expected to see me back quite so quickly, but it wasn't long before I was off again.

I walked along the *Millennium Route* from Spice Island to Gunwharf Quay alone.

It was a windy, overcast day and the forecast was for plenty more wind and rain.

It was going to be lively for the first couple of days.

I dragged my feet and stared at the pavement, with a frown on my face as I went.

The crews, with their family and friends all met up on Gunwharf Quay and the fleet was blessed at 0900 hours.

We kissed and hugged our families, before being rushed through the gates, onto the pontoons and towards our yachts.

One at a time we left the pontoons as our selected songs were played over a sound system as balloons were let go and streamers fired.

We got the sails up and waited around the starting area, designated to keep us and any supporters vessels clear of each other.

Time passed slowly.

But it passed all the same.

At 1400 hours the starting gun went.

We crossed the start line in the rain and began our race as the first yacht away.

The dozens of spectator craft, of all shapes and sizes, jockeyed for position as Team Stelmar supporters aboard the Ocean Scene went nuts, shouting, screaming and crying floods of tears.

This was it, we were off.

As we cleared the Solent and headed west we found ourselves dropping back the fleet to nearly the last boat, the spectators slowly fell by the wayside and we separated into our respective watches. By late afternoon, there were twenty knots blowing from south, south-west and the routine of sail changes and reefs, that was to become our daily life for the next ten months, began in earnest.

That first night the wind picked up to thirty knots, peaking at a maximum forty-five knots in a rainsquall, it was a baptism of fire for most of us. We had undergone months or even years of training, both as a crew and on an individual basis, but the reality of the race was slowly dawning.

As if to point out to us the gravity of our new situation, we first tore our storm staysail (which is fondly known as "bullet proof" because it is virtually unbreakable); we then experienced a call of "Man Overboard". Tim Wright, one of our two watch leaders, was working on the pitching and rolling bow, in the night blackened by rain clouds which obscured the light of the moon, when he tripped and fell over the guardrail.

Perhaps luckily, he was "clipped on" which meant that he was never physically separated from the boat. We had been trained to always connect our lifelines to the jackstay lines (plastic coated steel cables which are attached to various places on the deck). Nevertheless, he was literally over the side of the boat and being dragged along at eight knots in the cold grey water of the North Atlantic.

We had rehearsed for this situation many, many times but the reality is always far worse for the nerves than the rehearsal. He was recovered in no time, but we were all rather shaken. A *News Embargo* was quickly put in place by the skipper, which meant that we were not to report the incident, via e-mail or daily log to friends or family.

This was to be the first embargo of many.

Another incident that night demonstrates well the comprehension of some of the less experienced crew members when during a violent squall, whilst the deck was a hive of frantic activity, a head popped up from the companionway to ask Clive if he knew where the scissors were.

A more inappropriate moment to be looking for scissors would be hard to imagine.

This particular person was to re-appear throughout the entire trip, that comment was a definite clue as to their perspective on reality.

By midday on the second day, the wind had eased to between ten and twelve knots and stayed that way for the next twenty-four hours.

By Wednesday 6th October, we had clawed our way back up to fifth place. There was a low-pressure system developing off the Spanish coast and we were the most easterly boat. The decision was to position ourselves to the west of it, hoping to take advantage of the predicted northerly air stream so, with the kite up, we headed west.

We also rewarded ourselves with the first showers on board.

The following day, at 0100 hours G.M.T. the off watch were awoken with the call of "All hands on deck" as the wind had increased to thirty knots and the kite had to be dropped quickly. We scrambled out of our bunks, dressed in a hurry and headed up.

There seemed to be crisis after crisis on deck and the off watch were regularly called up. The difficulty with being called up from your sleep is that you didn't know what had happened and were kind of in a daze initially.

We could hear all the bangs and shouts amplified through the hull and sense the urgency in the voices, but they were muffled and it was not always clear what was happening.

We just got dressed quickly, ready for the worst and waited at the bottom of the steps in the companionway for instructions.

This time was straightforward though, the flanker (kite) had to be quickly dropped and retrieved and the Number One Yankee hoisted.

Afterwards, we were due on watch so we stayed on deck. I took the helm and with the exception of a half an hour relief from Nicko, stayed there for the next four hours.

The sailing was magical.

My favourite time aboard has always been the night time, tonight the sea was an inky black except for the white foam which we created as we crashed through the waves, whilst the stars were stolen from our view by the grey clouds above us, only occasionally peeping through.

It was a truly memorable experience as Stelmar pushed through the North Atlantic swell, totally at ease with herself, well balanced and beautiful.

Up until that moment, since the start gun fired, I had felt that this was something that was happening to me rather than something that I was doing. It now dawned on me that I was actually taking part in a Round the World Yacht Race.

I was beside myself.

You have to take your pleasure when you get it though.

We received an e-mail from Challenge Race office on October 8th which brought us back down.

There had been a problem as the fleet sailed through a shipping lane near the Isle of Ushant off the French coast.

The English Channel and South Western Approaches are a particularly busy shipping area with lots of passenger ferries, fishing boats, tankers and various other forms of traffic. There is a Traffic Separation Scheme in place to form a sort of Highway Code and the equivalent Green Cross Code is referred to as the T.S.S. (Traffic Separation Scheme)

The basic rule is that you should avoid crossing shipping lanes, but if you do you must cross the road from 'kerb to kerb', taking the shortest route across the shipping lanes.

It appeared that Barclays Adventurer, BP Explorer, Pindar, Team Stelmar, Team SAIC La Jolla, BG SPIRIT and Team Save the Children had crossed it at an angle and had therefore broken the Rules regarding the preventing collisions at sea. It was a protestable offence under the Yacht Racing Rules and

Spirit of Sark, being the duty boat for the day, were required to send a report to the Race Committee.

Spirit of Sark notified Challenge of the route taken and Challenge in turn, notified us of their intention to protest us all, in accordance with the Yacht Racing Rules.

Challenge business were intending to protest the offending yachts.

It was windy and learning how to sail the boat to its optimum performance and living aboard in high winds, as well as trying to keep the *slippy side down*, meant that we had violated the T.S.S.

We hadn't wittingly taken a shorter route; it is common practice to cross shipping lanes, just being sure to look both ways before stepping off the kerb and go straight across.

We were only just coping with conditions.

It was pretty rough.

We would have to wait until we got to Buenos Aires when there would be a hearing and an International Jury would examine the facts.

If found guilty, we could well be on the receiving end of a points deduction.

Not really something to look forward to.

Not something to dwell on too much though, there was a big job ahead.

Daily Log 8th October

Last night we picked up the edge of the low-pressure system that we had been looking for, which brought some favourable northerly winds. Downwind sailing is generally more comfortable than upwind, as the boat is a great deal more stable and moving around, both above and below decks is much easier for the crew. The wind gradually increased last night to about thirty-five knots before "Grunter" watch handed over to "Groaner" watch.

The wind remained fairly fresh from 0200-0600 hours and some great speeds were achieved.

This morning at 0600 hours when the watches changed over again, it was freshening some more and by 0900 hours we were square in the middle of a steady forty-five knot blow.

At this stage the waves were huge and some of the downwind surfing was enough to make me go weak at the knees. I struggled to keep the bow pointing down the waves, although when we went for the third reef, there was little choice but to come slightly up on the wind to enable the mainsail to be lowered. A couple of times being threatened with a breaking wave broadside on, salt spray and spume completely filling the air.

This is absolutely extreme stuff, but come the position schedule, spirits were lifted to see that we had gained on the leaders.

Rumour has it that the low-pressure system has now dropped a further 11milli-bars; anyone there now has a long night ahead.

Richard Parson
Team Stelmar

This was our first taste of rough weather and big seas.

We'd all sailed in windy conditions, but never surfed a 40 odd ton, steel boat in genuinely hostile conditions.

We came close to falling over loads of times.

I was pretty un-nerved.

I didn't know how much worse it was going to get or how long it was going to last.

I was helming and as support at the helm, I had Mike and Ruth.

I felt completely vulnerable.

Neither of them gave me any confidence at all.

They were actually sitting back, having a chat and enjoying the ride.

I was completely responsible for keeping this whole thing slippy side down, with no back-up to speak of.

If I got it wrong, it went wrong.

"Are you guys enjoying yourself?" I casually enquired.

"Yes, we're fine." came the agreed reply.

*"Well I'm ******* ******** myself!"* I yelled above the noise of the wind, rain and sea, howling and shrieking all around us.

They instantly sat up and started paying attention to what was going on around them, looking completely boggle-eyed as if they had woken in a panic, magnifying the intensity of my own eyes by ten times.

They still wouldn't know what to do when it all went wrong, but at least they were on their toes now and expecting something to go wrong, which is where I was coming from.

"Wake up will you!"

Clive and Nicko pretty much kept the navigation and weather routing to predictions and forecasts to themselves and we weren't really party to that information.

Clive would occasionally explain his thoughts and their reasons but that night I felt jittery and ill-informed.

During one of the headsail changes, Phil and I were *doing bow*. We were struggling with this sail, every time we got a little progress we got washed down the foredeck by a wave or the sail did and we ended up half over the side struggling to achieve anything.

Phil looked at me and said

"Do you remember all the folks at home saying, "So when are you going on your trip then?" almost like it was a cruise ship."

*"This isn't a cruise, it's a ****** ordeal!"*

We laughed and got the job done.

Whilst we were there, I also managed to slay some demons that live on the fore-deck in anything above 35 knots of wind.

There were lessons yet to be learned though.

Daily Log 10th October 2004

After the bawdy excesses of the first few days, the hangover finally had to come. From the gales that introduced us to the race, the wind speed dropped away to virtually nothing. The entire fleet lost virtually all boat speed in a high-pressure system just near Madeira. The leader board changed as the boats at the front of the fleet that went towards the middle of the course, slowed down to a crawl and those that followed were able to go either to the east or west of them.

Their tactics paid dividends as the miles slowly passed beneath their keels.

For 24 hours, the crew aboard Stelmar sat anxious and frustrated as they help-lessly watched the changes take place, only being able to achieve boat speeds of a couple of knots and in one one hour period, travelled just a single mile.

From the third place position of Sunday, we found ourselves in seventh and then eighth place as the daily race positions were relayed to us via race H.Q. or the daily chat show amongst the fleet confirmed. Frustrating times indeed.

Overnight on Sunday/Monday brought a change however and with the excep-tion of the 0200 – 0600 hour watch, brought the best days sailing to date as we approached the Islas Canarias. The wind picked up to a steady force four and the sun shone. The Genoa was hoisted, the crew stripped down to shorts and t-shirts and we ploughed along at speeds of between eight and ten knots in the Canarian sunshine.

The next tactical decision was already being contemplated as a dissipated high-pressure system, just south of the Canaries on the West African coast begins to elongate. Most of the fleet decided to head west of it into almost certain headwinds, whilst Stelmar, BG and Sark went for the far more risky eastern option, gambling on tail winds, which potentially are far quicker.

Time will tell whether the decision will pay off.
Richard Parson
Team Stelmar

There was a comedy moment when the satellite telephone sprang to life one morning.

Ring Ring! Ring Ring!

"Clive, the phone's ringing! What shall I do?"

"Umm!"

"Answer it?"

It was so alien to have the phone ring that nobody seemed to be able to understand what it was doing.

It wasn't a noise that we were used to aboard and it totally threw us.

Imagine not knowing what to do?

It's like the doorbell ringing at home and someone asking "I wonder who that is?"

"What do you think would be the best way to find out?"

Or when we were asked if we would like a hot drink.

It tickled me that in times of crisis we offered one another a *nice cup of tea* as if what we normally preferred was something other than a nice cup.

"Would you like a nice cup of tea?"

"No, I'd rather be poisoned by a disgusting cup, thanks!"

I always asked for a *Nice cup of coffee* I didn't always get one though.

As we neared the Canary Islands, conditions proved to be tricky.

We parked up.

Team Stelmar, BG Spirit and Spirit of Sark had gone more easterly than the rest of the fleet and had made a choice to pass between the Islands hoping to get some advantage of any thermal activity. BG and Sark went further east than us and it worked for them.

Unfortunately, it didn't work for us.

The wind dropped to the merest breath and we practically stopped.

It was hot, sticky and frustrating.

We were desperate to get out of there and get moving again and our frustrations began to manifest themselves.

In the uncomfortable conditions, the SUMO's started heating up.

We had worked through the initial stages of dealing with living with one another, now it seemed, we needed to establish some personalities and they are not always what you expected them to be.

One of the first quarrels was with the personal kit that we were all allowed.

We had decided exactly what we were going to take with us months ago and prior to each start, just to confirm the decision, Kate sent out the following list to everyone;

Warm legs:

(Portsmouth to Buenos Aires, Wellington to Sydney, Cape Town to Boston, Boston to La Rochelle and La Rochelle to Portsmouth.)

1 pair of La Chameau Boots
1 Pair of Henri Lloyd trainers
1 drysuit
1 set of foulies
1 set of mid-layers (jacket and salopettes)
1 set of HP thermals (top and bottoms)
1 set of light weight base layer thermals (top and bottoms)
Sailing shorts (to be provided by Stelmar)
Quick dry T-shirt (to be provided by Stelmar)
Underwear: knickers x 3
                crop top x 2
Socks: Sealskinz x 1 plus 2 others i.e. thin liners for use with trainers and boots
Hats: cap - will be provided by Stelmar, waterproof grey one provided by Gore-Tex, floppy sunhat (optional)
Gloves: personal choice - max 2 pairs
Quick dry towel
Personal medication

Personal torch/batteries/knife
Sunglasses - 1 pair
Swimming costume - not sure on this one?

<u>*Cold legs:*</u>
(Buenos Aires to Wellington and Sydney to Cape Town.)

As above plus
x1 extra set of thin thermals (top and bottom)
optional micro fleece if you feel the cold
Hat - windstopper thermal variety (these have been provided by Berghaus)
Gloves - Mitts/thermal warm ones (one pair are being provided by Berghaus)
Neck tube
Socks - 2 pairs Sealskinz plus 2 pairs of warm socks
          2 pairs of liner socks
No need for swimming costume on this one!

Pretty un-ambiguous you might think.

To contain this kit, we each had a plastic box allocated to us. They were racked up in the sleeping area, with a strap on to keep them in place during rough weather.

It wasn't very big, just big enough to keep your kit in, with a little space for some sunglasses and your luxury item(s).

As a principle, we were allowed to take one kilo of 'luxuries' which usually consisted of a camera, a music player of some kind or a book.

The bunks actually have proper pockets in them with Velcro seals, so once aboard some kit could be moved into your bunk and 'hidden' away.

Jackets used as pillows, socks hanging over your bunk drying, gloves in your jacket pocket, a book, diary, MP3 player etc. in the bunk pockets.

We could also fold up some kit and put them behind the *Curver* box, thereby making more room in it. Not cheating on the allowance, just being able to find what we needed fairly quickly rather than have to route through the whole box, crammed full, to find a specific item.

Often we were 'hot bunking' though, which meant that we slept on the high side of the boat, whatever that may be, therefore we had to shift our sleeping bags occasionally, to the higher side of the boat which helped in theory with the righting moment of the boat, being ever mindful of boat-speed.

Your sleeping bag, book, music player, diary etc. had to be carried across the boat before you went to sleep. You also had to tidy the bunk of the person whose haven you had violated by rolling their bag back up and replacing it later and by rolling yours up and putting it back on your own bunk, once you had finished with it... obviously.

Our clothing, sleeping bags etc. were all branded and bought out of the crew fund. We all had the same and there were no opportunities to take extra kit. The idea being, that we were literally all in the same boat.

We had discussed the matter at length at some of our team building sessions and it was felt that fairest way of ensuring that we all pulled together, rather than some look in envy at others who were dry and warm whilst others froze in the wet, was to stick to an agreed inventory.

Some of the crew could afford the most expensive technical clothing, some could not.

Some bought into the idea, others just took what they wanted aboard and didn't really care that they were breaking their own rules.

As the first leg developed, some people were coming on deck wearing additional t-shirts or socks occasionally; it was noted by other crew members.

Clive was reluctant to get involved and the job of 'Marshall' was adopted by Kate who had organised clothing and kit lists.

She was fierce, but good.

Newton was under suspicion.

When coming off watch, the first priority was to get some food inside us and then get some sleep as quickly as possible.

Most of us used our mid-layer jackets as a pillow. Newton had brought an inflatable pillow with him which was certainly frowned upon, but he was allowed to use it even though nobody else had one, on the grounds that it didn't weigh much.

He also brought his own moisturisers, sun tan lotion, ear plugs, skin creams and lavender oil.

Going to bed for Newton was a four act play.

First of all he needed to wash and moisturize, get changed, then he had to make his bed up which consisted of looking all over the boat to find stuff which had strayed from 'where he left it'.

A few drops of lavender oil later and his ear-plugs were inserted and his head gently placed on his inflatable pillow so that he didn't have to live in the same world as the rest of us.

He also required an early wake up call so that he could get ready in time and didn't have to queue for the heads. (Toilets) If going to bed was a four act play, so was getting up.

I scoffed my food, with second helpings if there were any, stripped off to my base layer, jumped into my bunk and strapped myself in whilst having no real regard for etiquette or hygiene.

Just eat, then sleep, cleaning my teeth when I got up.

The ear plugs seemed to work quite well for Newton though until one fell out and landed in Clive's open mouth in the bunk below.

Clive kind of got involved from that point and Kate and Paula eventually started going through Newton's kit before each leg to check that there was no cheating.

He wasn't cheating, just finickity.

I got to quite like the smell of lavender eventually, but it did irk me in the early stages.

Same with Newton.

I was still responsible for the media side of things for the team, but on alternative days, Sue would write a daily log.

Although the log for 12th October was due to be submitted by me, Sue offered to write it.

I declined her offer and sent in the following;

Daily log 12th October 2004

A Chunder Blunder

The morning of 13th October saw Team Stelmar near to Palmas, one of the Canary Islands, with no wind to speak of once again.
The watch from 0600 – 1200 hours had passed uneventfully enough with little wind and low boat speeds. Small zephyrs of breeze could be seen on the still water, as well as the occasional flying fish and dolphin as the Island remained in what seemed like the same position all morning.

One thing that is fairly common practice amongst sailors in such conditions, and has been for many generations, is to hoist someone up the mast to a better vantage point, in order that they can identify areas of more, or less breeze to either sail towards or avoid, whichever the case may be.

As the watch changeover occurred at noon, and with the midday sun beating down, a crewmember from "Groaner" watch was required to go aloft.

Now there are many criteria for selecting someone to climb the 95 feet to the top of the mast, but today a simple error was made.

The crewmember selected was one that had,

More or less, been suffering from motion sickness for 10 days
Was feeling unwell
Had just eaten lunch
Been un-communicative for the last half an hour
Had never scaled the mast before

Nevertheless, he was hoisted to the top of the mast to look for wind.

After a half an hour at the top and still being un-communicative, even though his primary role there was to communicate, his first clear call was "Look out below!"

Instinctively, instead of ducking for cover, all the crew on deck looked heavenwards, which was their second mistake, as they were soon to discover.

It might not seem funny to you, but for those of us below decks away from the firing line, in a manner of speaking, our day was brightened enormously as the contents of his stomach rained down on the deck above us.

The queue for the showers shortly afterwards was a source of much amusement for some and considerable embarrassment for others.

Tee Hee!

Richard Parson
Team Stelmar

When I came back on deck at 1800 hours on that day, Sue told me that she had written the days log, even though we had discussed it and I had already filed the report with Challenge Race Office as they were to be in on schedule to keep the website up to date.

Sue was unhappy with things, although she made no explanation as to her reason or intent. As far as I was concerned the log had been entered, it was her turn tomorrow.

That was the end of the matter.

Not for Sue who reported the matter to her watch leader, Tim Wright.

He wanted a word with me.

I listened interestedly as Tim began asking me to keep him informed as to which logs I was submitting, whether I had any that I was holding back for a day or two, how I should write them and what their content should be.

It didn't take long for me to become disinterested.

I explained that I would not be happy with that situation, I had been editing and filing reports from the team since February and felt that I was doing a reasonable job. I didn't mind if someone else wanted a go, but I was damned if I was going to let her take it on without having my say.

The following day, it was Mike Morgan's (my watch leader) turn to have a word with me.

The conversation was very similar but this time I held my tongue and when

Mike had finished his piece, I told him that I would consider his opinion and report back to him with mine in due course.

That comment brought me before Clive.

Sue, Clive and I went to the foredeck to have a private chat. Obviously everyone on board was fully aware of what was going on, they all had an opinion on the matter and most would share theirs with you.

It was like eighteen radios on transmit, with none of them on receive.

In my opinion, if we had to go through this process every time somebody did something that Sue didn't like, it was going to be a long race.

I listened to Clive telling the pair of us that we would need to work together, understand and compromise with one another and he made all the right conciliatory noises.

Then I listened to Sue complain that in her opinion, I thought that I was *in charge* of media, she wasn't happy that I had edited some of her longer reports and wanted more say in which photographs were submitted to Challenge.

"There we are," said Clive, "so if we're all happy, perhaps we can try and avoid this sort of thing in the future, work together and compromise. Okay?"

"Erm. No. I'm not okay." I began,

"As far as I'm concerned, there is no problem here except with Sue. She asked me if I wanted her to write the daily log in my place, I declined her offer. I am happy to continue being *in charge* of media, but I will only take instructions from Clive (who occasionally asked me not to write about certain events) and Nicko (being my cohort since February). I will decide and edit which logs are reported, I will select the photographs to submit to both Challenge and our own team websites, I will keep the crew profiles and news postings on our site current, I will take photos of the whole race including stop-overs and I will collect all the team photographs and make sure that everyone gets copies."

"Sue will answer to me."

"Back me or sack me."

I'm pretty sure that was not the response that was required.

We suffered the worst by going between the Islands; the others had managed to maintain some boat speed whilst we floundered for nearly two complete days on Tuesday and Wednesday 12th & 13th October.

The boats behind caught up and the boats in front pulled out a bigger lead.

The wind came back but the delay had cost us.
We were still in ninth place but at least we were moving again.
There were other problems in store though.

Daily log 15th October 2004

For the last three days, we have been enjoying the absolute best conditions for sailing. The wind is behind us, blowing at something between force three or four and the spinnakers have been flying. The wave height is such that we are able to get an occasional ride on the surf that it produces, meaning that the boat speed will occasionally reach fourteen knots. It is absolutely idyllic.

The only problem is the D&V that is gradually working it's way through the entire crew, one at a time.

One of the problems with eighteen people living in such close proximity to one another is the fact that coughs and sneezes as well as other complaints, spread like wildfire.

The average family home usually consists of a couple of bathrooms shared between, on average, four people. Think of the wet towels that they produce, together with the clothes washing and the hair that lurks in all the plugholes and other those hard to reach places. Now multiply that by five and take away the washing machine and any room to dry and air the towels. Beginning to get the idea?

Hygiene is absolutely paramount especially in the warm, humid conditions that we are experiencing.

I realise that it may be cold and wet at home but the humidity does have it's drawbacks too.

Richard Parson
Team Stelmar

During the day on Friday 15th October, as we sailed down the North African coast, we started noticing debris in the water. It looked like dead leaves from a tree, but logic told us that it couldn't be. There weren't very many trees around here.

It wasn't long before a locust flew into the mainsail and fell down onto the deck.

Uh Huh!

The wind was blowing from the east and it quickly became apparent that

a swarm of locusts had been blown off the African coast and were now dropping exhaustedly into the ocean, or on Team Stelmar.

Initially, Paula and Newton started trying to feed them sugar to revive them
and set them up for their return flight.

Slightly myopic if you ask me, besides which, I'm sure that there would be
plenty of African farmers that would be delighted to see them where they now
were.

Once they started appearing below deck as well as above, all friendships
dissolved and all charity dried up.

We made a determined effort to rid ourselves of them.

As we sailed through various time zones, we had to adjust the ships clock
to keep up with them.

Invariably, as we were travelling *West About,* we had to lose approximately
an hour a week, which meant that we had three times to consider.

Greenwich Meantime, Local time and Boat time.

To optimize this opportunity, we put the clocks back at 1200 hours on
Sunday, which meant that we could all eat together on deck without either
watch losing time on deck, or off it.

We had our first fancy dress party on deck on Sunday 17th October.

The theme was The School Disco.

In true schoolboy style, I took both Kate and Paula as my dates.

Also in true schoolboy style, the relationships didn't last any longer than
the disco. Once they realized that I had asked them both, there were arguments.

Nothing serious, they both thought that I was a rat!

Unfortunately, they didn't fight over me.

The fancy dress parties carried on when it was practical but they were only
once or twice on a couple of legs, rather than every week.

It was a good way to break the routine of watches and sailing, eating and
sleeping.

Days have no meaning, you're either on watch or you aren't.

Because of the way the watches were arranged, one day you were on deck
from 0600 – 1200 and off from 1200 – 1800 hours and the next day was the
opposite.

You either have a six hour morning watch off, when you can probably sleep
because it won't be too hot that early in the day, or you have the afternoon watch
off, when you were generally allowed a wash and could write an e-mail or two
but there's practically no chance of any sleep and you'll be sweltering in your
bunk for hours, wishing we could pick up the cool trade winds once again and
get moving.

Sleep was important, but dreams were frustrating.

Keeping in touch with home, via e-mail messages was also important but it distracted you.

Both had their advantages and drawbacks.

Mainly it was sail, sleep, eat … and sometimes argue.

Occasionally Clive nominated a volunteer to speak on a specific subject.

The volunteer then had three or four days to swat up and would deliver their lecture on Sunday, again if conditions allowed.

Usually the talks were facts about something relevant, like a land mass or an Island we were passing or birds or sea life that we were seeing regularly.

Not exactly a sermon, but delivered on Sunday.

It was a good way to distract us from our pettiness and look at what was all around.

I learned some interesting facts and I continue to use a similar idea with some friends to this day.

We were racing though and the Equator crossing was imminent and the passage was on our minds.

We were approaching the Doldrums.

The sailing was going to be tricky, but there might be some opportunities if the leaders slowed up as they hit the light airs.

We could do with an opportunity.

Daily Log 19th October 2004

After over fourteen days at sea, the fleet are making their steady progress towards the equator and the doldrums or "horse latitudes". (So-called because in years gone by, the old sailing vessels would sometimes jettison the horses aboard, knowing that the light winds and calms would make it too expensive to feed them and keep them alive).

Although the fleet is currently split over nearly three hundred miles, with Stelmar nearly one hundred and thirty behind the leaders, the notoriously light and fickle breezes at that position make crossing through the doldrums a risky and often painstakingly slow process. (Tradition has it that the first time a sailor crosses, he or she should make some kind of offering to Neptune, the God of the Sea. Look out for funny court cases and carryings on!)

The yachts towards the latter half of the fleet will be watching the leaders extremely carefully in the hope that they will "fall into a hole" in the breeze and thereby offer an opportunity to be overtaken or at least for some very expensive miles to be gained, knowing that once through, there is little realistic chance, except by some error on the leaders part, of making any significant gains on the final run down the south American coast towards Buenos Aires.

The other potentially costly obstacles to be encountered at this stage are tropical thunderstorms, which can bring fierce squalls at very little notice which potentially mean damage for the boat and/or crew and lost miles or speed. Sometimes these dense black rain clouds can be spotted on the ship's radar and there is opportunity to prepare for them by reducing sail, sometimes not!

I speak from experience. Shortly before 1830 hours on Tuesday 19th, Stelmar encountered just such a squall and whilst the downpour could have been welcomed as a cooling down opportunity, the effects of the breeze was not!

With so many miles to go, there is still opportunity for some exciting racing!

Richard Parson
Team Stelmar

The squall that we encountered peaked at twenty-nine knots. We broached, tore the flanker and broke one of our two spinnaker poles.

It was Keystone Kops sailing at this stage.

We had been monitoring a squall on radar and were concerned that it was going to pass immediately overhead.

At the time, we were flying the race kite which is bigger and lighter than the flanker and therefore would not be strong enough to stand the wind strength if the squall hit. When it became obvious that it was going to hit us, instead of simply dropping the race kite and preparing the 1.5 ounce kite (which is very similar in size and weight to the race) to be hoisted once the squall had passed, we went for a much more risky option of replacing the race kite with the flanker and crossing our fingers in a hope that the squall wouldn't get above thirty knots, which is the maximum wind strength for the flanker.

It hit, the boat went over on its side and chaos ensued.

On decks everybody was shouting something, almost anything really and scrambling around or simply hanging on.

Below deck, Groaner watch were thrown around in their bunks.

They quickly dressed to try and help out and were asked to go to the forepeak (front of the boat) to collect the damaged sail. Then they were asked to come to the companionway (back of the boat) to collect it from there, then to the forepeak, then back to the companionway.

They were running up and down the length of the boat, we were scrambling around on deck, shouting and trying to regain control.

It was not a polished performance.

There were no injuries though and the flanker was repairable, although it would take a week-and-a-half. The broken spinnaker pole was a different matter.

When gybing the boat, we needed two poles, otherwise we would have to drop the spinnaker, gybe the boat and then re-hoist another spinnaker.

We couldn't repair the pole; we would have to make do with one.

The trouble was, each kite (or spinnaker), would need to be dropped now before a gybe.

It would then have to be re-packed before it could be used again, a process which involves tying the 'legs' with wool and putting the main body in a sock, before methodically packing the whole thing in a bag. When perfected, the whole process usually took about a half an hour.

It was going to affect our speeds and taught us a valuable lesson.

It was disappointing.

Careless.

Daily Log 21st October

Its 0600 hours on Thursday 21st October. Team Stelmar is situated at 5 38 67 N 27 46 73 W which is typically well within the area known as the Doldrums. We have just come off watch after 4 hours, all the time looking for favourable winds, whilst tracking storm clouds and rainsqualls on the radar.

The lighter weight spinnaker has been hoisted and retrieved many times, as has the genoa (headsail) and we are all suffering from the stifling heat. The only reprieve being an absolute downpour from one of the squalls passing overhead, which, whilst it cools one down, also jangles one's nerves constantly as we wait for a sudden, dramatic increase in the wind and another sail retrieval and re-pack, followed by more of the same.

As soon as we come off watch, the wind backs to the direction that we have been hoping for and whilst we are delighted that the yacht is now sliding towards Buenos Aires once again, we can't help feeling a little cheated that we did not enjoy it whilst on deck.

The conditions are likely to endure for the best part of another week, by which time, I wager, we will all have become nail-biters!

The pressure has manifested itself in many ways, one of which is the "Weird Beard" competition. Although open to all, the girls are currently reluctant to enter into the spirit of things, whilst some of the guys are not giving anything away but apparently intend to trim and shape at the last minute. Phil, however, has leap-frogged his way into an early lead by fashioning his entry very early on.

Richard Parson
Team Stelmar

Most of the guys were enjoying the fact that they didn't need to shave, but it was too hot to have a full beard so we started fashioning beards into weird and wonderful shapes. It formalized into a competition, open to everyone, to be judged at the Team Stelmar meal in B.A. once we got ashore.

It was getting warmer aboard and as we went through the hot and sticky times, the inside of the hull started dripping with condensation, it was nigh on impossible to get any air moving below decks and the smell was unpleasant.

We were all tired and had grown through the initial, exciting phase of living together in a close, impersonal environment. There was a certain amount of settling in going on and that meant putting down some limits.

Ones that you cannot easily legislate for.

Frustrations were raised on 21st October when a casual comment from one of Groaner watch let slip that they were using small hand-held fans to keep cool in their bunks.

We had bought nine of them in England before we left and had agreed that, as they were battery operated and we did not have enough re-chargeable or standard batteries for constant use, we would limit the time they were available by agreeing when we wanted them issued.

They were hidden away somewhere until either Kate or Clive issued them and then they would be shared with your opposite number, there being only nine fans and eighteen crew.

The thing was, reportedly, that it wasn't a secret that personal fans were in use. Oh no, these were not the boat ones to share, these were specifically for Groaner Watch as Flash's mum had given them to him.

We weren't told, but it wasn't a secret.

Stupid thing to get worked up about really, but it was hot and sweaty and we weren't doing very well in the race.

The fans weren't much use.

When you lay on your back in your bunk with the fan in your hand, blowing cooling air on your face as you drop off to sleep, you drop off to sleep and your hand drops.

Brrrrr!

Ow!

Wide awake and lying in a sweat sodden, canvas bunk.

Still sweating, but with a blister on your nose.

I was obviously beginning to see the funny side.

As well as the stomach cramps and sickness that had affected most of us by now, *Yottie Bottie* was making an appearance. Due to the fact that sailors are constantly in damp and humid conditions and personal hygiene standards get relaxed, they develop sores and spots on their backsides.

It is a common complaint and Dr. Ruth was prescribing, but refusing to administer, cream to help.

Whilst slightly uncomfortable, it is nothing more than a minor irritation and we coped, mostly.

Ruth later found it necessary to designate surgery times as it seemed that everyone wanted her, most of the time.

If there was a trauma or injury, obviously she was called on, but if you had yottie bottie or heat rash like Rob and I, it was only fair that it could wait until she was getting ready to go on watch or at least actually awake.

We had watch meetings during our time at the lunch table, after having completed the morning watch. (i.e. every two days.)

It was a time when we knew we were rich in terms of the amount of time we had off watch, being unable to sleep because of the heat.

Dr. Wil had produced a target looking graph which we had stuck up on the notice board. It was a dartboard looking graph, segmented as well as numbered.

Each of the segments dealing with the various aspects of how we rated our performance to date.

We then scored ourselves marks out of ten in each field.

After that, we each then had a thirty second rant in the S.U.M.O. meetings (Speak Up, Move On) and that helped us confront each other's difficult behaviour, or different approach, in a relatively un-confrontational manner.

We needed to get a grip on ourselves as a team, to know that we were being Safe, Happy and Fast.

We also needed to learn to discuss things that were puzzling us about other people's behaviour.

By now everyone had begun to take their responsibilities seriously and sometimes we were either a little misunderstanding, or being misunderstood ourselves.

We spent too much energy looking at everyone else and not enough looking at ourselves.

What we needed were some real problems.

One day, we were told that we had run out of butter, only to discover that we hadn't actually run out, run out.

We had more butter, but we were saving it.

Not everyone knew that.

The situation was bordering on the ludicrous and my log tried to reflect my opinion.

Either we had run out or we hadn't.

Daily Log 23rd October

The butter has run out.

Well, when I say run out, it's not strictly true, although that is the official line.

In fact there's plenty of butter left, it's just that we're not allowed to open another tin for two days. You see the normal packets of butter ran out on the day before yesterday and so we had to go to the tinned stuff.

Nothing wrong with that.

The only thing is, when we reckoned on how long a 250g tin would last 18 people, someone figured 3 days and nobody questioned it. That meant that when, after one day, when we had used the first tin, there was to be no more issued for two days.

Should we eat it now and lighten the load that we are carrying, hence opting for the "Boat Speed" option or eke it out so that we can have bread and but-ter when we arrive in B.A?

The Squirrel option.
If you lose count of the days, do you miss your rations, or can you have dou-ble the next day?

The Cunning option.
As the watch system is worked out on a forty-eight hour period, is there a bias towards one watch or another because they are awake longer and eat their meals first, or is it better to eat second, so that you can dig deep into the tin knowing that you're not depriving someone else of their daily ration?

The Pedantic option.
Does the daily watch start at 0600 hours watch or 0200 hours?

The Guts option.
Will the opposite watch consider you, or will they tuck in knowing that there is no more for tomorrow and what they don't eat, you're going to finish any-way?

It certainly is a puzzler and whilst nobody else aboard has shown the slight-est signs of concern, due in part to our imminent arrival at the equator, I hope we don't run low on toilet paper!

The other thing that was still really *p******* me off was that people were sleeping on deck whilst they were on watch.

When challenged, the usual culprits denied that they were asleep and learned to wear sunglasses or claimed that they were only resting their eyes.

Okay, sometimes it was slow on deck and there wasn't a lot to do, but you owed it to the team to remain alert, as far as was possible and try and help out in any way.

As far as I was concerned, when their heads were nodding and they were snoring, they were asleep.

If they weren't, they certainly weren't adding to the team effort.

I brought it up at the SUMO but Mike (my watch leader) disagreed and the subsequent conversation went something like this:

"I really think that falling asleep on deck is a crime!" I said.

"Well there are times when it is okay." Mike replied.

"No there aren't. We are supposed to be racing. When we're not looking out, we're relying on other people to look out on our behalf. Even if you're too tired to think, you have to keep your eyes open."

Mike replied. "I'm telling you that it is okay."

"That's because you go to sleep too and you know full well that it is wrong." I said.

Maybe I wasn't dealing with life as well as I thought that I was.
We had a long way to go.

At 0846 hours (local time) on Saturday 23rd October 2004, we crossed The Equator.

For all of us, apart from Clive, it was the first time.

A good opportunity to take our minds off the pettiness and bickering.

There are various shenanigans that go on there and have done for generations of sea-farers. It is supposed to make you realise that you are in for a rough time.

These days it is a watered down version of bygone days, but it could be considered unpleasant.

Unpleasant enough to concentrate your thoughts.

Daily Log 24th October 2004

Saturday 23rd October began with Alex's 34th Birthday, a theme that was to re-occur at every watch changeover during the day, which could have brought his tally up to 37 years by midnight.

Apart from that, the day was rather eventful;

We crossed the equator at approximately 0845 hours, local time. The event is usually considered to be significant and this time it was no different. Myself and Ruth had specifically requested to be woken from our bunks, in order that we could be awake and at the chart table to see the instruments record the fact that we were passing into the Southern Hemisphere.

It is traditional for virgin "equator crossers" to make some form of offering to King Neptune to thank him for granting safe passage from North to South. The most accepted ceremony on board a Challenge yacht is to have a court hearing, whereby each individual is tried for some misdemeanor and found guilty. The usual punishment is to be covered in some kind of foul concoction. I'm pleased to say that this passing followed the traditional form and we were ceremoniously "glooped" by King Neptune.

Following the formalities, Dr Ruth started unpacking various medical packages and boxes in preparation for her first scheduled morning surgery. Things have been getting rather unstructured in the minor ailment department, Yachtie bottie, heat rashes, various skin complaints etc. and although she is happy to give advice whenever she can, some things can wait until she is awake!

Today though, there was an appointment for Nicko. He has been suffering with a slight cyst (which had become infected) on his leg and it was about time to do something about it, so Dr. Ruth, Nurse Wrighty and "Box Lid Holder" Kate set about preparing the galley. Needless to say I was there at every step with the camera and the patient's permission to record events. Everything went according to plan and he was ordered to take some rest, the same order that he has been given for many days, this time however, he did go to his bunk for a while. Ruth commented later that the surgery had been very quiet since then!

The afternoon watch brought the company of first one, but later more, Gannets. These expert fishermen fly slightly above deck level and, as flying fish are disturbed by the boat, casually pluck them from the air. Gannets reportedly eat as much as they can until they can't fly and have to digest before they can start again, hence the expression "Greedy Gannet". These particular ones didn't quite get to that stage because they continually emptied their loads, in a manner of speaking, over both yacht and one particular crewmember! (Not this one!)

Watch change over brought some more "Gloopings" from King Neptune and *more birthday celebrations for Alex, including a cake baked by Phil, another chorus of Happy Birthday and the additional news that we were making up places in the race meant that we all slept a little more soundly.*

Happy Birthday Alex!
Rich Parson

Nicko had a slightly more than minor irritation which he had reported to Dr. Ruth.

He had developed a cyst on his leg, which was playing up. Ruth had given it some attention and during her *Morning Surgery* on Saturday 23rd October, she dug into his leg to remove the gunk. (My words, not hers.)

The operating table was the galley table and Dr. Ruth, Kate (as a physiotherapist) and Wrighty (as a former psychiatric nurse) robed up and prepared the patient.

I grabbed the camera, hoping to see some old fashioned, heavy-handed patient restraint from Wrighty that I could report on.

All I saw was Ruth removing a load of debris from a hole that she had cut into Nicko's ankle and him wriggling a bit as it happened.

The incident wasn't reported at the time to avoid undue concern from Nicko's parents. He spent the next three days below deck with his leg elevated and in some discomfort.

He was still able to navigate though and is a restless patient; he was back in no time.

Phil, who was on Mother Watch, had baked the cake for Alex as it was his birthday, but due to the fact that we were sailing at an angle of about 15-20 degrees and that Phil had made the mixture too runny, it came out wedge shaped, with the thin end burnt and the thick end not cooked in the middle.

Good Phil, but no cigar.

We all got better at that. We taught the leggers too eventually.

The wind picked up and came forwards, for the first time in over a week; we dropped the spinnaker and later even put the first reef in the mainsail.

We had passed through the Doldrums and were now, well and truly, in the Southern Hemisphere where water goes the other way down a plug hole and more importantly, where weather pressure systems rotate in the opposite direction.

As the wind increased and came forward, we began to make some good progress towards the Brazilian Coast.

Overnight we passed Imagine it. Done. which placed us in eighth position.

At least with the wind forwards and the headsails up, there were no mysterious holes appearing in the kites and we could concentrate on the outstanding repairs.

It didn't last though and before long, the wind backed and blew from behind us once more, which meant that although we could point in the right direction, we would be flying the kites again.

We were still in the process of repairing the flanker that we had torn in the squall nearly a week ago.

The wind was due to increase, if it was sufficiently strong, we could go straight to a *poled out yankee** and would not lose out.

If it didn't, we were vulnerable.

(*Using the one spinnaker pole that we did have, to hold the edge of the Number One Yankee on the opposite side of the boat to the mainsail. A similar effect to using a kite but more stable in the upper wind ranges.)

This time, we had a little luck.

The wind increased and blew 20 – 25 knots for the next two days, sometimes gusting higher. We couldn't risk using the kites available to us, but it was sufficiently windy to use the poled out yankee.

By Wednesday 27th October we were flying along.

The sun was shining and there was a warm wind from the north.

The sea was a beautiful clear blue and the skies were uninterrupted by clouds.

Stelmar pushed through the water, occasionally hitching a ride on some of the one metre high waves that were running at us from behind.

Flying fish leapt out of the water on our bow as we heavily crashed in on them.

The speeds crept up.

We knew we were doing well when we received the position schedules and were able to compare distances that the other yachts had travelled and the current fleet positions.

Over a twenty-four hour period, we covered two hundred and fifty-nine nautical miles.

The fastest boat in the fleet over a twenty-four hour period.

We had now started living up to the fast part of the deal.

On 28th October, with the exception of three-quarters of an hour break, I helmed the entire 0600-1200 hours watch.

Rob was on Mother Watch and he was our other helm at that stage, so I *drove* for almost the entire watch.

It was fantastic sailing.

We planned to continue on our course towards the coast and rely on the weather forecast, which predicted the wind to lift our current course and enable us to potentially save a lot of miles if we got lifted around Cabo Frioo in Brazil.

Most of the rest of the fleet were taking a more conservative route slightly further offshore, if our risk paid, it could make us some gains.

By the time the predicted lift came, we had been forced to tack because we were already too close to the coast, it meant that we had to tack onto a terrible course and cost us more miles.

Imagine it. Done. passed us.

Dammit!

Of as much concern was the fact that we were now in company. Brazilian fishing boats started to make an appearance. If we could see land, land could see us.

The real concern off the Brazilian coast is Pirates.

Obviously any boat could contain pirates and was not identifiable as such. It could be organised gangs in high speed rigid inflatable boats (RIBS) or opportunists, such as fishermen. They would be after our passports, credit cards, medicines, anything really, see what they could find.

Sir Peter Blake, a famous yachtsman, was murdered by Pirates whilst onboard his yacht SeaMaster in the Amazon Basin on 5th December 2001.

It was unsettling to have another boat make it's way towards us.

We were used to being alone; the world's oceans are surprisingly devoid of shipping or vessels.

I felt that they were sort of crowding me, just by being in sight.

My attention was soon diverted though, as my log at the time reported.

Log Entry 29th October

This morning we were sailing along nicely with Brazil to our right and our spinnaker flying in front of us. T-shirts and shorts were the order of the day as we slipped along with the wind slightly abeam, blowing a steady 12 knots, sunshine on our faces.

Idyllic conditions.

Shortly after watch change over at midday (Local time) a squall passed overhead and the wind rose sharply from 12 knots to approximately 18 knots. The planned spinnaker change was aborted and the genoa hoisted instead. By 1330 hours the wind had risen to approximately 25 knots and all plans were changed. By the time I got back on watch at 1800 hours, we had over 30 knots "on the nose", three reefs in the mainsail and the number two Yankee and stay-sail set. The boat was heeling at an angle of approximately 25 degrees and although I was still wearing t-shirt and shorts, they were well covered up with a dry suit, life jacket and boots. The discarded, unpacked spinnaker lay at the bottom of the steps near the galley, as did the Genoa. The storm jib, which was undergoing some repairs, was spread out over the galley table and someone was being sick on deck.

It was like stepping up onto the right planet but at the wrong grid, so far removed was one from the other.

Richard Parson
Team Stelmar

All of a sudden, things could be a struggle on deck. Events were happening quickly and squalls would hit us violently.

On 29th October in the midst of such a squall, whilst wrestling some sails from the sail locker, Tim Wright took a tumble as the boat lurched, fracturing two ribs as he fell heavily against the side of the door frame. After a bit of attention and about an hour in his bunk he could stand it no longer and had to get up on deck to help out.

It wasn't until later, when I saw the x-rays in Buenos Aires, that I really gave him full credit for how uncomfortable that must have been, or how well he dealt with it.

He went up in my estimation.

He jumped up in fact.

I still didn't have a U.S. Visa.

I had my original interview at the United States Embassy on 22nd June 2004.

It was really bugging me.

Weeks after the interview, I had a reply from NSY; there was a problem with my application. The two "Proof of Identity" documents weren't satisfactory,

I had to send them again.

It turned out to be a really expensive oversight.

I took all the correspondence with me to the London Embassy but they weren't happy with it.

I was told that they would look into my application and I would be informed, in due course, of their decision.

I pestered them a little, but not too much.

When we left Portsmouth, I had no visa and no decision from them on what was likely to happen next.

Then the visa application rules changed.

Now, if you were applying for a U.S. Visa, they needed a finger scan as well as all of the other stuff.

I was technically, still in the process of applying.

Even though I had kept my fingers crossed that I wouldn't have to fly home, they wanted me back in London for another interview and they wanted me to bring my fingers with me.

My Mum and Dad and my respective Step-Parents had been working with Tina and Vale Sesto to try and sort out an appointment that meant I could fly back from B.A. and return in time to re-join the boat for the next leg.

If the application was unsuccessful or they wanted to make further inquiries, they could withhold my passport, which would be disastrous.

There was no news of any appointment yet.

Besides which, I didn't have any fingerprints to bring with me. They were spread throughout the weave of the various sheets, halyards, winch handles and wheel cover on the boat.

I would love to have brought them with me as it would have meant that my hands didn't hurt as much as they did, but I couldn't and they did.

I would just have to take what I had, if and when I got an appointment.

We were sailing downwind a lot of the time and that meant a reasonably flat boat, good speeds and spinnakers flying.

The trouble was, we were tearing the kites regularly and were at a loss to discover the cause.

It felt like every time we flew one, we tore it.

They were only little snag holes but they had to be attended to immediately, before the rip-stock nylon ripped all along a whole panel.

A stitch in time and all that.

We had sat staring at them from all angles for hours.

We had climbed the rig and collapsed the sail on purpose to see where it was touching.

We had taped over every conceivable place on the rig where we thought there may be a snagging point, but it kept on happening.

It was a constant concern.

Daily Log 2nd November

Sod's Law, Murphy's Law, Tempting fate, call it what you will, but with less than seven hundred miles to Buenos Aires, the skippers aboard the challenge yachts are (quite rightly) insistent that all talk of estimated arrival times is not allowed. (That doesn't stop a little, unofficial sweepstake from taking place amongst the watches.)

Yacht racing is a peculiar business and, as we are keenly aware, the wind doesn't always do what we expect it to. One day of light and floppy conditions could hold everything up; likewise a decent blow from the right direction could hurry things along a little.

Sail damage, on the other hand, is always a potential problem and could seriously hamper all efforts to a swift arrival.

Since posting the last report, "Grunter" watch awoke to find two spinnakers laid out in the galley area with no substitute to use until repairs had been made. There are a total of twenty-two repairs in our race spinnaker at the time of writing. Each repair takes valuable time and reduces our effective sailing speeds meaning that the competition either pull further away, or catch up which ever the case may be, yet we are at an absolute loss to discover the cause of this headache.

Whilst the whole fleet have had their problems, we are really only concerned with our own at this stage in the game. We have just come off watch with the warning ringing in our ears that we may be called back on deck at any minute to assist in any way.

The race kite is currently flying!

With "Me to You" breathing down our necks and "Unisys" in our sights once again, don't think of the finish or the ETA.

Instead, when you have read this article, close your eyes, cross your fingers and say as loud as you dare "COME ON STELMAR!"

Richard Parson
Team Stelmar

It seemed like every time we hoisted a kite, we discovered a rip or tear in it so it had to be dropped and repaired. I hated re-packing kites and with the exception of being on Mother Watch, can't think of anything that I would spend more energy trying to avoid.

Almost anything rather than that really!

We had tried so many things to discover and eliminate the cause of this problem, but with no success. When we arrived in Buenos Aires, we discovered that most of the fleet had suffered the same frustrations.

It turned out to be the new fittings on the intersection between the mast spreaders and the steel stays.

A simple leather collar eventually solved the problem.

"4 years ago the sail makers spent approximately 650 hours repairing sails. This time it may be as high as 750 due to the conditions."
Andrew Roberts – Challenge Business Technical Director.

Huh!

On 2nd November the wind picked up and we went to poled out yankee once again, we passed Imagine it. Done. and re-took eighth place.

We had over thirty knots of breeze and achieved a top speed of sixteen-and-a-half knots.

The wind continued to build on the following day when it peaked at forty knots and we made our way into the mouth of the River Plata towards Buenos Aires.

In places the river is only six or seven metres deep and with a one metre swell, it was pretty hair-raising.

The water is very rich in mineral and ore deposits and it is a very brown river, which is pretty much unmistakable in colour.

The hazards are usually, but not always marked and the ones that are marked are usually, but not always lit.

We hoofed up the river at an average boat speed of eight knots all through the night, dodging Traffic Separation Schemes lawfully and finally crossed the finish line at the Yacht Club of Argentina in Buenos Aires at 0742 hours (local time) on Thursday 5th November maintaining our eighth position.

I got drunk. Very drunk.

Everyone had quite a bit to drink that day.

The following day, work began on the boats.

I had an appointment for the U.S. Embassy in London on Tuesday 9th November.

I worked on the boat for a couple of days and flew back to London, arriving on Tuesday morning.

My Dad had driven all the way from Plymouth to help and was waiting at the airport. He's an absolute tower of strength, support and understanding and had already had his own epic journey to get to be there waiting for me.

This was the latest in a long list of occasions were he has driven miles to help out with my sailing activities.

We hugged one another.

It was great to have my Dad.

We made our way to the Embassy.

We were far too early!

They interviewed me, scratched their heads as to the lack of decent finger scan pictures, dismissed me and kept my passport, promising to return it, together with a decision, '*in a week*'.

That meant I could go home and wait, Yeah!

Dad and I caught the tube back out to Hatton Cross and jumped in the car.

Three and a half hours later, I jumped out of the car and got squashed with a bear hug. I had been looking forward to that for a long time.

Tina was looking gorgeous, her hair had been dyed a different colour and was re-styled. She was wearing new clothes and had been training hard at the gym. She looked fantastic.

Dad dropped me off and then drove himself home, his day wasn't finished. He had helped me more than I could thank him for.

I obviously said thank you, but he just kept on putting himself out.

He had been awake for twenty hours, had driven all the way up and back to collect me and bring me back, helped out at the U.S. Embassy and had been a tower of support throughout.

All things considered, it was an extreme effort.

On 10th November, whilst I was still in the U.K., the Protests were heard in the Yacht Club of Argentina.

BP Explorer, Spirit of Sark and Stelmar were found to be in violation of Rule 10 of the International Regulations for Preventing Collisions at Sea.

Rule 10 relates to Traffic Separation Schemes. Rule 10 (b) (ii) states that "A vessel using a traffic separation scheme shall: so far as is practical keep clear of a traffic separation line or separation zone". Further, Rule 10 (c) states " A vessel shall, so far as practical avoid crossing traffic lanes, but if obliged to do so shall cross on a heading as nearly as practical at right angles to the general direction of traffic flow".

All three were deemed to have spent a prolonged period within the zone and subsequently received a one-point penalty. The hearing was controversial because the protest was brought by the race committee (technically being unable to lodge a protest if the violation was not noticed by them, but as a result of information passed on to them by another competitor). A very similar protest involving seven yachts and an earlier violation was rejected by the International Jury for this very reason.

Also, Spirit of Sark were awarded a thirty minute penalty for using both of their spinnaker poles at the same time for a period of more than four hours, effectively making the boat much more stable as the spinnaker cannot roll around in the same way as it does when it has a non-fixed edge.

Rule RRS 50.2 was contravened.

Rule 50.2 states that "Only one spinnaker pole or whisker pole shall be used at a time except when gybing...."

If you were cynical you may think that it would be a convenient way of solving the kite snagging on a mysterious object when it collapsed problem.

They reported it to the Race Committee themselves though, so it sounds like an honest mistake.

The penalty had no effect on the leader board.

Whilst I was at home, I met Tina for lunch most days, as she was working during the day. In the evenings, I drank too much and I couldn't sleep or settle.

Most of the time I passed out on the sofa, while she lay awake in our bed.

Together, we caught up with as many family and friends as we could, I attended the gym with her a few times and we went out for a meal with her new training partner, a guy called Keith.

We had known him, from the gym, for ages.

He was her new best friend.

Her mum was pretty cosy with him too.

Within five days I received my passport and visa.

I flew back to Argentina.

The Southern Ocean was next.

As a team, we had plenty to discuss in Buenos Aires.

Clive had organised a team building session where we could sit down together and discuss the various issues that had arisen on the first leg and some of the issues that we could face on the coming leg.

There had been too many minor issues on the first leg that had been disruptive. We would have to focus more on putting up with other peoples' behaviour and concentrate more on our overall performance.

Things hadn't been going well with Mike Morgan, Grunter's Watch Leader whilst I was at home either.

He didn't attend the session.

Some issues had come to a head between Ruth, Adrian, Paula and Mike during the leg and again during the stop-over.

Mike and I shared a room when I got back to B.A. and he and I had spent a lot of time together in the early days of the team, he told me his version of events but the important thing is that he decided to leave the team.

He flew home, leaving a letter on my bunk to give to Clive.

We only had four days until the race re-started. We were heading for Cape Horn and the Southern Ocean one crew member down.

He was one of the physically tougher ones as well.

We could have done with Mike and his strength.

Dammit … again!

One of the things that I was pulled up on was being grumpy whilst on Mother Watch.

Newton had heartily agreed with this point and had announced that "…you'd think we wanted blood out of you if we ask for another cup of tea!"

I was relaying the tale to Tina later on the phone and she said;

"Well, that's something you can work on in the next leg isn't it?"

"Yes!" I replied, "Newton's attitude!"

At the Prize-Giving in the Yacht Club of Argentina marquee on 25th November, Team Stelmar won the Rubber Chicken Award for the most humorous log.

The log which I entered about Tony throwing up from the masthead entitled 'A Chunder Blunder' had spread a bit of fun.

It had appeared in a couple of the yachting magazines at home.

We picked up an award at the first prize-giving and the score sheet was opened.

Ha!

Leg Two – Buenos Aires to Wellington.

(Leggers - Karen Smith and John Campbell)

On the morning of race day, I had agreed to phone Tina at home and say whatever people say on these occasions.

The entire crew were due to meet up early for breakfast and once we had eaten, there were various formalities and ceremonies which took place on or by the boats including crew photographs and a ceremonial blessing of the fleet, so we had a pretty full agenda.

Besides which, we were all completely pre-occupied with thoughts of the coming leg and nerves about the start.

I was to phone before breakfast; we had agreed a time so that she would listen for the phone.

Time and again I rang and rang but just couldn't get through. I became more and more agitated as time passed and slowly it dawned on me that I wasn't going to be able to get through to her, nor was I able to concentrate on matters at hand.

I had visions of her thinking that I hadn't bothered or I had forgotten, when it fact, it was driving me nutty trying. I couldn't get through to her though so I left in a bit of a dither.

She stopped sending me e-mails for the first four days, eventually she did write but things weren't right and I knew it.

We didn't start particularly well, we were the tenth yacht away, but by Tuesday 30th November, we were back up into sixth place and in contention.

Conditions were idyllic as we sailed downwind in 10-15 knots of breeze, gybing occasionally in the warm South American sunshine.

The temperature dropped steadily though as we headed south.

Problems ashore didn't exactly disappear, but they faded away.

Daily Log 29th November 2004

At 1400 hours local time on Sunday 28th November, the 2004/5 Global Challenge Yacht Race was re-started. Although two boats were deemed to be OCS (On Course Side i.e. over the line as the start gun fired)

Dozens of spectator craft waited just beside the starting area and hooted and cheered as we got underway in the afternoon sun.

For the crews, the days of beer, beef and bed linen, which have been enjoyed for the last three weeks, were replaced with the routine of life on board. In 15 knots of breeze the sails strained and the talk was of little else but sail trim, boat balance and the lack of mosquitoes, which have been the bane of our lives for the last couple of weeks. We were off, out into the River Plate and the journey towards the infamous Cape Horn and the Southern Ocean was begun.

Overnight on Sunday, we were all within sight of one another and in a beautifully bright moonlit night, we counted the masthead lights again and again as we imagined ourselves gaining slightly on that one, or losing slightly to another. The wind dropped away and as we drew closer to other yachts, all conversation was barely above a whisper in case we could be heard and our game plan discovered.

Shortly after midnight, we increased the amount of sail that we were flying by dropping the Number One Yankee and Staysail and replacing them with the Genoa, a ploy that, although not visible under the cloak of darkness, was undoubtedly repeated throughout the fleet.

Constantly we monitored and adjusted sail trim, always looking to eke another fraction of a knot of boat-speed over our fellow competitors and make some slight gain in position.

The game of Cat & Mouse was begun.

Richard Parson
Team Stelmar

I had read plenty of sailors' accounts of rounding Cape Horn and the sea state that the Southern Ocean can conjure up and of course there were the tales from the last race and the horrific injuries sustained by one of the crew on board Veritas (#43).

There was also plenty of footage on the Challenge video/DVD set, which I had watched so often I could almost recite the lines spoken.

As Mike had been a 'Grunter' our watch was the one to lose out initially, as we were reduced to seven crew members. Rob changed watches and Alex came over to us and was made our new watch leader. (If you take the Navigator and Skipper away, each watch consisted of eight members.)

The rough game plan once we left Buenos Aires was simple. Sail the 100 miles out of the River Plata, pass three waypoints and head south.

We quietly settled back into life on board, most of us nervous about what could be coming our way.

We picked up where we left off, but now we were much more mindful about how difficult it could be for us, without petty bickering to complicate matters.

Keep Safe, keep Happy and keep Fast.

I was having difficulties in my approach to 'Mother watch' still and had gained a reputation of being surly and miserable whilst doing so.

Mother Watch consisted of mainly staying below deck and cooking and cleaning for the rest of the crew. I have very little enthusiasm for cooking and food preparation at the best of times and have a complete lack of imagination or aptitude in that department which doubtless went some way towards explaining my demeanour.

After breakfast on Thursday, I was on Mother clearing up the breakfast dishes and washing up. Ruth poked her head down and reported that Newton would like another cup of coffee. (Or was it de-caffeinated tea, tea with honey, lemon tea, or one of the fruit teas that had appeared? I can't remember.)

My response of *'Well, Tough!'* hung in the air as I looked at him and he looked at me.

The difference was, he wondered whether I would accommodate him.

I didn't.

It was tough.

I had other jobs to do and the request was prioritized.

Suffering Sockatash!

The wind changed direction as we sailed further down the coast and the southerly breeze not only made sailing more uncomfortable as we bashed into the swell, it also was blowing from Antarctica and therefore was cold.

It was like someone leaving the freezer door open. That was the last time for quite a while where we would be able to wear T-shirts and shorts on deck.

On Sunday 7th December when we were twenty-five miles from Cape Horn and all thoughts were of rounding it, Clive called a meeting on deck.

It had been superceded by Dr. Ruth asking for everyone on watch to go up on deck whilst she made some satellite 'phone calls to Dr. Spike Briggs (from Challenge) and the Casualty Department at Derriford Hospital in Plymouth, who were helping out with medical advice.

The upshot of the meeting was that we were going to have to go back to South America to drop Karen Smith off for urgent medical attention.

Regrettably, we were not told why she needed to be dropped off and although she was obviously upset about having to go back, any physical symptoms of an illness were not obvious.

The nearest port was Puerto Williams in Chile.

We turned back.

Stelmar were a great help and together with Vale Sesto and Challenge, everything was organized for us to drop Karen off in Chile where medical attention would be waiting for her.

We headed along the Beagle Canal into one of the world's most dramatic areas, to meet the Chilean navy.

Karen was a popular crew member even though she hadn't spent long on the boat.

She had introduced herself to the team back in Portsmouth before the race started, so it felt like she had been involved with the project for a long time.

We really didn't want to lose her.

She was a lively and happy girl and we could have done with her.

We turned the boat around and headed back.

As is etiquette in these matters, we are required to fly the flag of the country which we intend to enter. Clive is a stickler for observing such etiquette; the problem was that we weren't scheduled to stop in Chile.

We obviously hadn't packed everybody's flag, just in case.

Necessity is the Mother of Invention though and Julian rose to the challenge.

Having been born in Chile, he was familiar with the flag; a piece of Dacron (sail repair material) was commandeered and utilized. He proceeded to draw it using the coloured marker pens and 'Hey Presto!' one Chilean flag.

In no time at all it was flying proudly from the spreaders on the mast and we were motor sailing up the Beagle Canal on our final approach to Puerto Williams, arguably* (very arguably, it turns out) the world's southernmost town.

(* The other is Ushuaia in Argentina. They watch each other along the length of the Beagle Channel all day and all night. The Argentinians in a kind of glossy gold quilted Parka, the Chilean's in black, with dogs and sunglasses. Both armed, obviously.

The Chilean's scare me most. They look meaner and they spend a whole lot more money on defence.)

We approached Chile in a somber mood and moored alongside a Chilean naval launch in Puerto Williams, where we were boarded by members of their navy.

They were certainly very helpful and after we had all hugged Karen and somebody had given her some Pesos which they had left over from our stop-over in Buenos Aires, she was whisked away in an ambulance for medical attention.

The Chileans were impressed with Julian's flag, so much so that they asked to keep it, in return they took down the flag which was flying from the launch and presented it to Clive.

We all signed ours and Clive presented it to them with our grateful thanks, I think it ended up in the town hall.

If you're ever down that way, I would be interested to know whether they kept it.

We were only off the race course for nineteen hours and before long we were on our way once again.

At 1400 hours on Monday 8th December we rounded Cape Horn in forty knots of wind and a large swell running.

Unfortunately, it was so grey and miserable that we couldn't actually see 'the Horn', but it was academic really, we had seen plenty of the coast of Tierra del Fuego and the Beagle Canal, Cape Horn was just a small part of that.

We shared a bottle of champagne amongst the dwindling crew and I wrote a message with our contact address on and created a message in a bottle with the empty.

I launched it over the side, but I'm not holding my breath to hear from the finder.

More than likely it ended up on the rocks.

For the next three days we battled upwind in up to 45 knots of breeze.

The Beagle Canal and Tierra del Fuego is surely one of the world's most dramatic places. Nothing had prepared me for the absolute desolation of this part of the world. The mountains and coastline are grey and foreboding, capped in snow even in the height of summer and with the odd glacier thrown in for added effect, it really rocks you on your heels.

As we rejoined the race, we changed our plan; the new plan was not to be the last boat to Wellington.

We picked up a new gauntlet and ran with it.

There was some discussion as to whether we would be able to claim redress for the time that we had lost off the race course and as I was involved in the 'rules council' (together with Clive and Nicko and various others that knew what they were talking about), I e-mailed Tina and asked her to approach a couple of friends of mine at home and ask them for their opinion.

As it could be regarded as outside assistance to be getting information from off the boat, I also made it clear that she wasn't to reply with any information, just acquire it and I could speak to her when she arrived in Wellington.

Unfortunately Tina simply forwarded on my e-mail to everyone in my computer address book. That included Challenge Business staff, amongst others.

I had already asked Clive if I should send out such an e-mail, so when he accusingly proffered a print out of an extract from it and asked me if I'd sent it, I was slightly surprised on two counts.

Firstly that Tina had been so unhelpful and secondly that Clive seemed unaware that anything had left the boat.

Because I had made it clear in the e-mail that she wasn't to reply, we weren't exactly in trouble, but it wasn't the attention that we wanted.

Clive e-mailed Challenge distancing himself and the team from the content and I resolved not to rely on getting help from anyone too much.

Then I had another turn at Mother watch.

It wasn't getting any easier for me as my log of 9th December reported.

Daily Log 9th December

Rise and Shine!
It's just after 0200 hours on Thursday morning; it's another cold, grey day here in the Southern Ocean. The wind is still blowing at 25 knots and there is water coming over the bow as the boat rides through the huge swell.

I am on mother watch. As usual, before waking properly I visit the heads, only to find that during the night, the constant slamming of the boat in the waves has smashed the plastic container of hand-soap and the contents are now liberally spread all over the starboard heads. Brilliant!

Worse still, because of the angle of heel (varying from 20-35 degrees) we are unable to produce any water. Other than the emergency supply, we have about half a tank, which is not enough for the day, so there's only seawater to clean it up with. That has to be carried through the same, still pitching and bouncing boat. I close the heads to the rest of the crew, some of whom are trying to get on deck, some of whom will shortly be trying to get to their bunks after four hours on deck, most of whom want to use the heads.

Any minute now, my watch will be looking for a warm drink to keep the cold at bay, there's breakfast to prepare and we're two crewmembers down.

I'm shining as brightly as I can this morning!

Richard Parson
Team Stelmar

We began to make some decent progress once more and by Tuesday, we had moved up into eleventh place and were only one hundred and twenty miles between us and the lead boat.

In twenty knots of wind, we were achieving between ten and twelve knots of boat speed. It was fantastic to be right back up with the fleet and making such good progress. Our efforts paid off when the position report schedule (sked) came through from Challenge on the thirteenth of December, we were in fourth place.

A remarkable comeback.

The weather was atrocious now and hail, rain and huge seas battered us, as the wind relentlessly kept Stelmar 'on her ear'. Working on deck, particularly on the bow, was dangerous and for the first time we began to realize what the Southern Ocean was going to let us have.

It was daunting.

Nobody was ready for what happened next.

<u>Log 15th December 2004</u>

Shortly after 0730 hours on December 13th, whilst in the process of falling asleep heaving completed the 0200 – 0600 hours watch; we were woken with an alarming call.

"Man Overboard!"

We had completed dozens of emergency scenarios during training, but judging by the tone of voice, this was serious. Quickly and quietly we dressed and

*prepared ourselves to get on deck. There was no unnecessary shouting or call-
ing and very little talking amongst us. In times like these, all non-vital communication needs to be kept to a minimum in order that vital stuff can be
heard above the noise of the wind and the waves. The training had paid off.*

*Stelmar had already been turned to run downwind to steady her off, Clive was
on deck overseeing things and we were ready below decks, waiting for
instructions. Dr Ruth quickly ascertained whether she was required above or
below deck, Phil donned his dry-suit as he was the designated "swimmer"
should one be required, the galley table was cleared and the kettle put on to
boil.*

*Inwardly, we wondered what had gone wrong. We didn't have to wait too
long to find out.*

*Tim Johnston (aka Flash) was gently lowered down through the fore-hatch and
we gingerly carried him to the galley table ... he had been "dumped on" by a
huge wave and smashed against the forestay whilst working on the bow.
Almost certainly, his left arm was broken; we couldn't tell if there was any further damage until Ruth had had the chance to make a more thorough examination.*

*Once on the galley table, his dry-suit and inner clothing was cut off and we
were able to make him comfortable while Ruth methodically and thoroughly
went about her business.*

*His left humorous was indeed broken and after some consultation with Dr
Spike Briggs and Derriford Hospital Casualty Department, the decision was
made that he needed to receive hospital treatment within a week. We were
approximately one thousand miles from South America and more like three
and a half thousand miles from New Zealand. We had to turn back.*

Another "No Brainer".

*Rich Parson
Team Stelmar*

A *'No Brainer'* was Clive's expression; it meant that we didn't really have
to think about a decision.

It was obvious.

There had been a news embargo for a couple of days when Tim's parents
were informed and Challenge could get to know the facts of the matter before

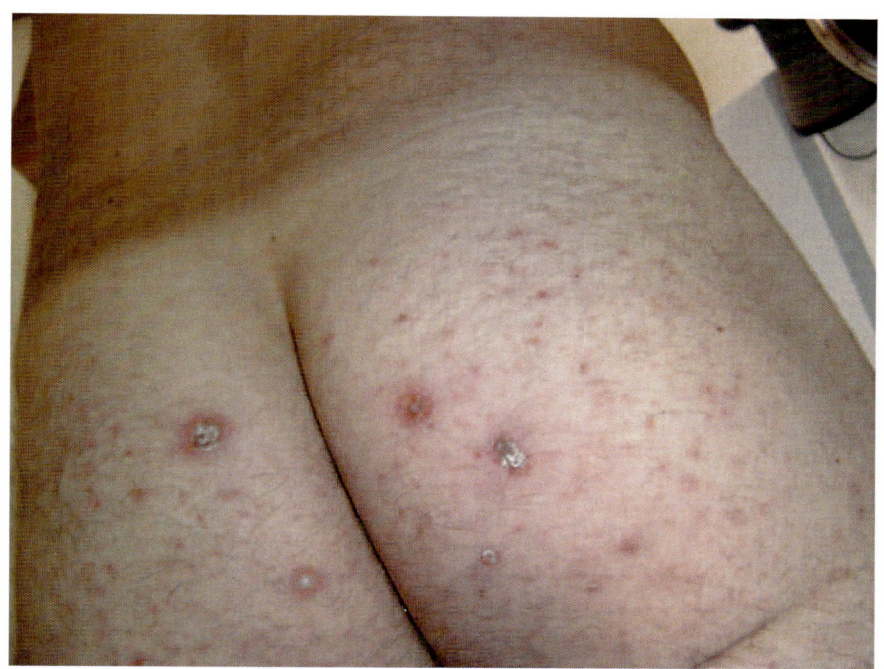

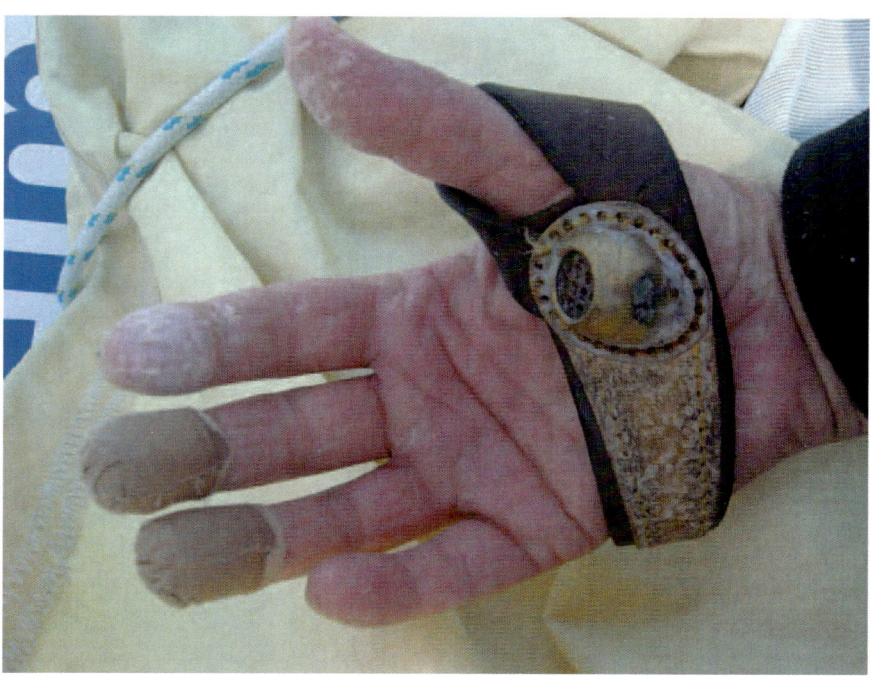

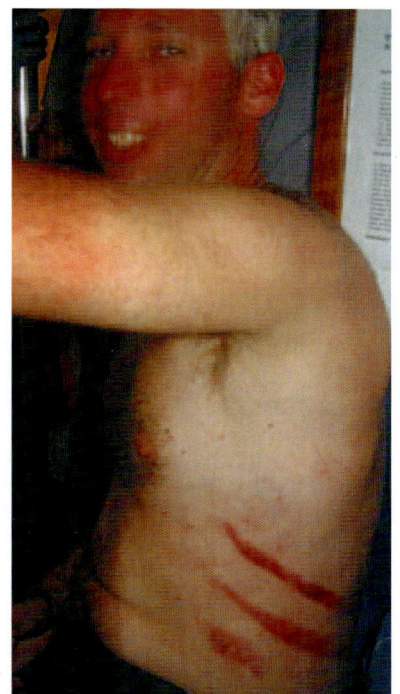

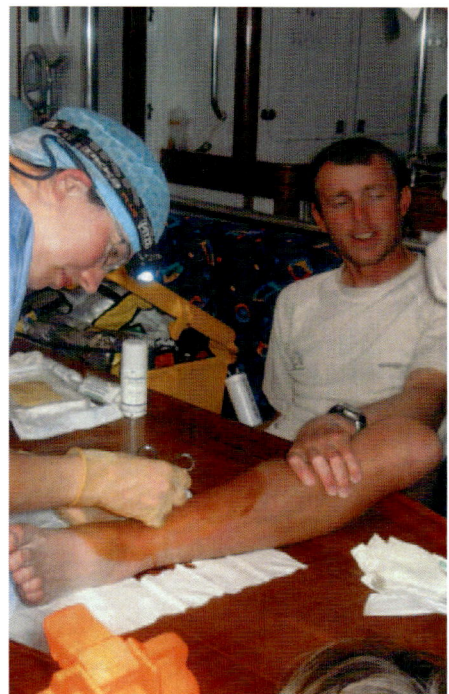

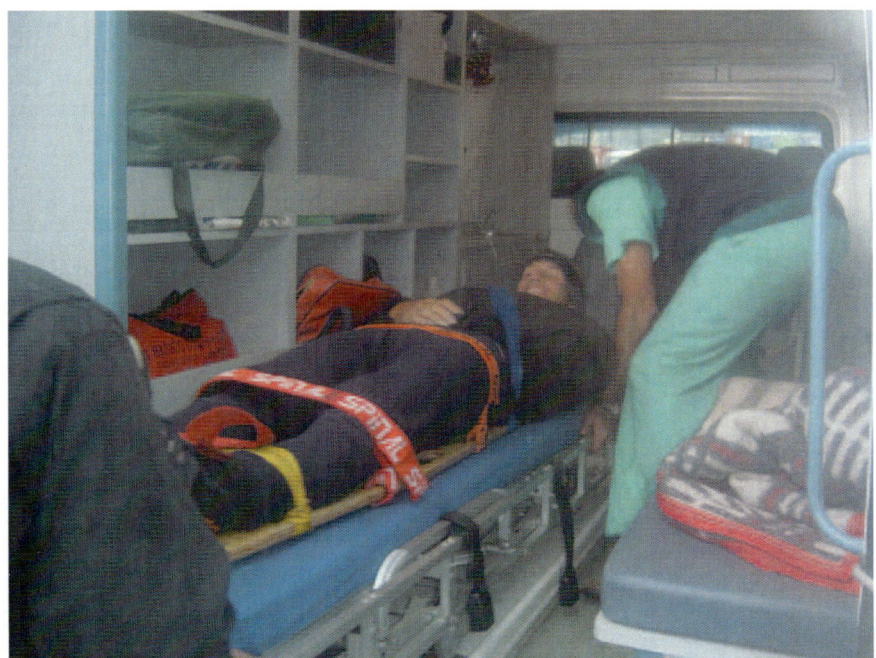

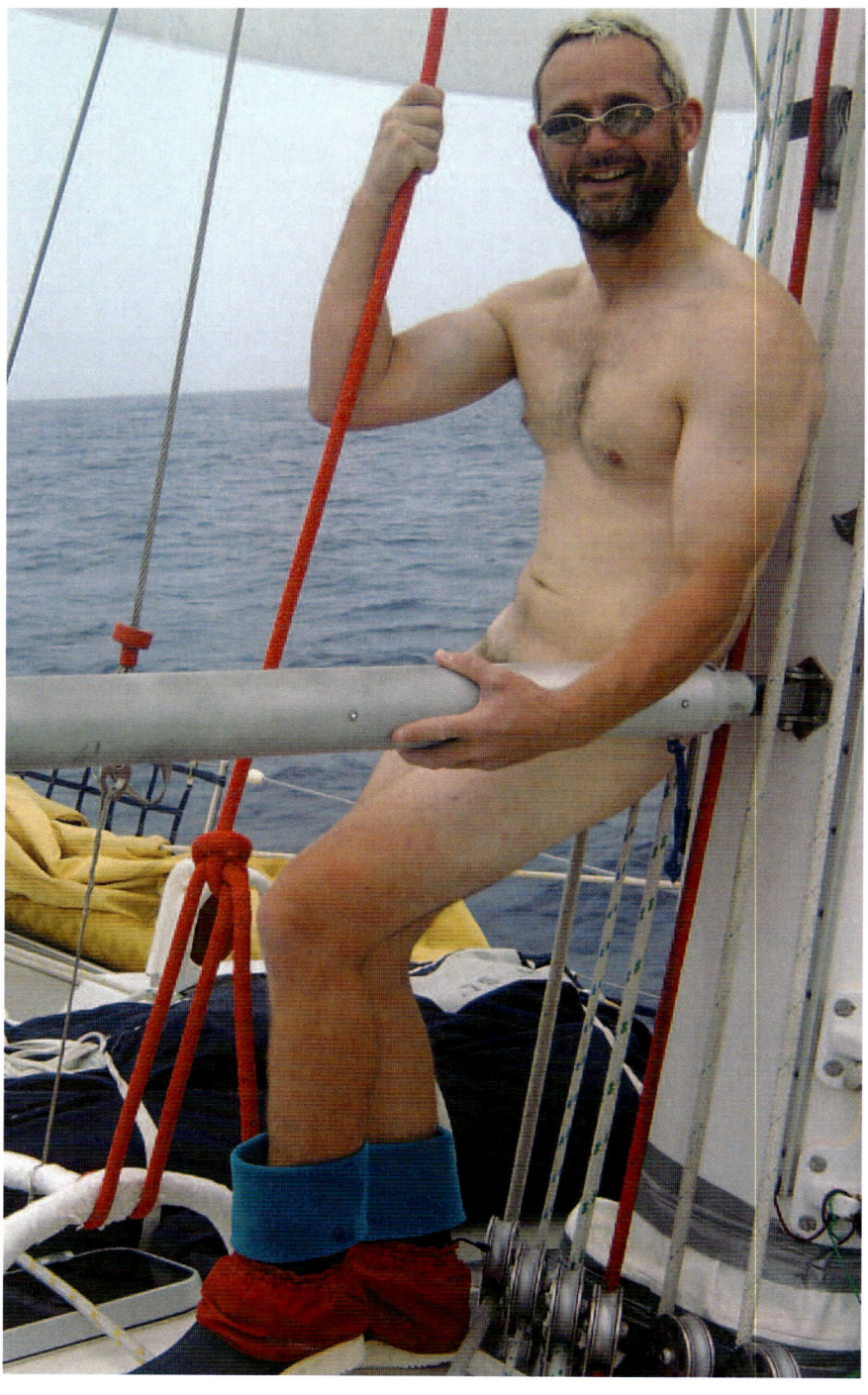

making an announcement. It was important to get it straight and avoid undue speculation from all and sundry.

In the meantime, we were heading back for a thousand miles, towards Tierra del Fuego and Cape Horn, which would eventually place us 2,000 miles away from our safety net which was the rest of the fleet.

With its notorious reputation, Cape Horn couldn't be more desolate.

Lashed by gales and storms for thousands of years and the last resting place of scores of mariners.

It is every bit as dramatic as you can imagine it.

Going back alone was scary.

Flash was made comfortable once we had carried him below deck.

We laid him on the galley table and propped him up on it using various sleeping bags etc. as the roll of the boat was such that he could easily have fallen off it had we not been vigilant. As it was, we had bumped him along the sides of the boat as Phil and I struggled to carry him along the narrow passage between the fore-hatch and the galley. His clothes were cut off him and Ruth made a more thorough examination.

His arm was definitely broken, but also of concern was the fact that he was suffering from pins and needles in his hand. That could mean that his nerves were damaged, which wasn't good news.

Ruth did what she could and he was strapped up. Once he was comfortable, he was moved to my bunk with the bunk above it being removed so that he could be propped up.

In normal use, I couldn't lie on my side in my bunk without my opposite shoulder touching the underside of the bunk above and therefore poking into the person resting in the bunk above.

Removing the higher bunk meant that he could be propped up and we could get to him to administer pills and play cards with him.

Ruth, Kate and Wrighty were responsible for Flash's medical care, but everyone tried to help in any way that they could. Paula went as far as rigging up a bell of sorts with a drinking mug on deck, secured to a piece of string which passed through a hatch and dangled down to his bunk.

He yanked the string, the cup rattled, people came running.

Clive spoke to Challenge Race Office on the Sat C phone on 16th of December.

It was a private conversation, but their recommendation was that we should retire from that leg of the race and motor-sail to Wellington.

My daily log read as follows;

Daily Log 19th December 2004

… You could be forgiven for believing that giants live here and not the Big Friendly variety of Roald Dahl, more the Jack and the Beanstalk type. Mean, monstrous types that eat Englishmen for breakfast.

The "Challenge of a Lifetime" that is the Global Challenge Yacht Race is shaping up to hold many unexpected twists and turns and this is just another in a series of incidents that we are experiencing.

We now find ourselves in the unenviable position of having to travel the four and a half thousand miles to Wellington alone, out of this stage of the race, three crewmembers down and with very little prospect of any real R&R when we arrive.

We are currently drawing up a schedule of events to occupy our time during the next month or so, including physical training, Yacht Racing Rules seminars, working practices and procedures reviews, breakfast meetings, Yachtmaster classes, weather routing, plans for legs three and four, in fact a whole host of plans to ensure that we fill our time in a constructive manner.

We may be down at the moment, but we're still on our feet and we intend to come back …soon.

Richard Parson
Team Stelmar

Approximately an hour-and-a-half after the actual incident, we had reported to the race office our intention to suspend racing. Between then and the time that we started the engine, we sailed the boat downwind to keep it as level and as stable as we could whilst we could properly assess our situation. Therefore, we were still sailing technically.

Once we had notified the Race Office, we were at liberty to start our engines as we would not be technically sailing. We didn't start the engine however until much later and therefore we potentially had three potential "Waypoint Flashes" to which we might return, in order to possibly re-start racing in the future.

Where he was injured and we turned around, where we reported to Race Office and where we started the engine.

We were required to return to that point after dropping off Flash, if we were to continue with the race, or risk being disqualified under the Yacht Racing Rules.

There were other things to consider, as well as dropping Tim off. Amongst other things, we had to calculate the amount of food and diesel we would need if we were to attempt to cover an additional 2,000 miles. We would need to re-stock, the trouble was, if we did that, we may be disqualified for receiving *Outside Assistance* in the race.

If that was the case we wouldn't be technically racing and we could head a much more northerly route and avoid the worst of the low pressure weather systems that roll through the Southern Ocean, concentrating on preserving the boat and crew.

We were now about to be three crew members down, with one less, we would be disqualified under the Class Rules.

If we carried on with the leg and finished in last place, we would receive four points; if we retired from that leg we would receive three points.

We needed to decide whether to continue racing or not.

We still had that decision to reach though and help was at hand.

Chay Blyth sent us some words;

Chay's Letter (16/12/04)

The Global Challenge is certainly a challenge. We have seen in the past some major damage to yachts and severe injuries to individuals. What we have also seen is how the crews respond and get over their adversity. You on board Stelmar have certainly had your share of adversity with two Medivac situations.

Soon you with Clive will be faced with a choice. The options are to return to where you stopped racing. This has powerful ongoing other potential challenges. For this you will receive 4 points for 12th position. The second option is to discontinue racing, take a more northerly and, in theory at least, a more forgiving route. It will still be hard. For this you will receive 3 points for retiring – one point less that if you had carried on racing.

Within this equation and, to my mind, probably more important is the focus for the next and subsequent legs – there is the time factor for the preparation of the yacht in Wellington to consider. The more time spent there preparing the yacht will ensure your competitiveness for Leg 4.

You will have questions and by discussion amongst you the answers will come through. If they don't then contact me.

My personal belief and what I would be doing and expecting if I was to suffer in such a situation would be expecting us all to be on the same team. To concentrate on getting the yacht and its crew to Wellington as fast as reasonably possible. To prepare and focus on the remainder of the race.

You cannot win the Global Challenge Race now but you certainly have the potential to win legs. This was evident when you were catching up the fleet after you dropped off Karen.
Good Luck and a safe berthing to get Tim off.

Chay.

We had another meeting on deck and following some discussion, Clive announced his decision to go along with Challenge's recommendation and retire from leg two.

When reports started appearing which stated that we had decided to retire from the race, I felt that it didn't matter what we thought, the decision had been made and we were simply to go along with it. The only other time that we had had a democratic decision, it was over-ruled by Clive. I held little hope of being able to convince him to go along with the majority, if indeed it was to swing towards pressing on.

The following day was a different matter. We had another meeting on deck and due in part to the e-mails which we were receiving from home which urged us to continue and at least attempt to get to New Zealand before the cut off time period.

We agreed.

We changed our minds and decided to continue racing the leg.

It was a defining moment.

Skipper's comments

Tim 'Flash' Johnston is undoubtedly one of our strongest, fittest and most dedicated crew members, whether it be working on deck in his thermals when he should be sleeping, climbing the rig to untangle a wrap or at the end of the pole to spike the kite in a squall he was always there. On leg one we coined the phrase, 'Flash does the hard work so you don't have to'.

We will miss him and his enthusiasm, but are all very grateful that despite his injury he is in high spirits and once again consuming large quantities of chocolate. He receives regular visits from us all, keeping him updated of events elsewhere onboard. We have even started taking pictures on the digital camera to report back to him with, most recently our electrical tape Christmas tree.

In a few days now we will be dropping him off to seek the attention he needs. This will undoubtedly be an emotional time for us all, but we are Team Stelmar and we will continue as an ever closer team.

Clive Cosby Skipper

Daily log...15th December

Here are a few words from the man himself...

'It's been over 2 days since I broke my arm on the fore deck. The painkillers are doing a great job of numbing my arm but unfortunately they don't do anything to ease the pain and frustration caused by having had to turn the boat around and head back to Chile, especially when we had been doing so well. Clive and Ruth have been utterly professional in dealing with events since the accident. I've just read Rich's article about the accident and can confirm that my crewmates did a brilliant job of bringing me off deck and patching me up, to the extent that I haven't felt at all worried about being injured so far from dry land.
Despite the huge disappointment for all of us the crew have maintained their great support and sense of humour throughout this latest setback. Paula has even set up a pulley system for lowering chocolate bars from the cockpit through the hatch above my bunk – I am certainly being very well cared for! We have been greatly lifted by all the goodwill messages we have received from family, friends, supporters and fellow competitors. Many thanks to everyone who has written messages of support.
The events of the past couple of days have made me feel even more proud to be part of Team Stelmar. I'm gutted about having to leave the boat but I'm already looking forward to rejoining my crewmates as soon as my arm has healed.
There are a lot of very determined people on this boat and we will appear at the top of the leader board again – I want to be back on board when it happens!

To my crewmates – keep your heads up and have a safe trip to Wellington. I'll miss you all over the next few weeks but I'll be waiting for you in NZ with a crate of beer. Save a Raisin Yorkie for me!

Tim 'Flash' Johnston
Bowman, Team Stelmar

Daily Log 16th December 2004

Life on board has settled into a very different routine as the primary objective is now to 'race' towards South America and get him sorted out ASAP. The hourly log is now supplemented with 'Flash' checks as Ruth, our medic, and myself check on his arm to make sure there is a strong pulse and sensation is intact. Pain control is of the highest importance and Flash has already become expert in self medication...the pink pills are currently favourite! Flash appears settled in his new bunk with chocolate bars readily accessible.

Kate Stainsby

Flash wasn't an expert in medication, he just liked the look of the pink ones!

A bit like Smarties or Penguin bars, they may be different colours but they all taste the same.

Not everyone wanted to carry on though and some felt strongly about retiring for various reasons.

Several of the crew were disillusioned.

Once we turned back for the second time, it became obvious that the predicted arrival time in Wellington was going to be way out.

As we were due to be staying there for about four weeks, many had family and friends travelling from the U.K. to enjoy a holiday and spend some time with us, since the last time we had seen most of them was four months ago.

We had also faced the Southern Ocean and some massively uncomfortable seas for the first time in our lives and we faced thousands more miles before seeing land again.

We were already longing to hug a tree or to lie on some grass and look at the sky.

Paul 'Bubbles' Goodman was suffering with elbow problems and was in some considerable discomfort, many of his family and friends were planning on making the trip.

He was missing them and couldn't bear the thought that the re-union was in jeopardy.

He discussed his fears with Clive in private and reached the decision to leave the boat once we arrived back in South America.

His plan was to fly to New Zealand and meet his family. When we arrived, he would re-join the boat for the rest of the race.

Paul phoned his wife Karen on the Sat C telephone and told her of his decision. She asked him to leave any travel plans to her and to phone again later and she would report on progress. When he did speak to her later, she informed him that she had cancelled his credit cards and he was therefore stuck with us.

There was no way he could make any plans when he got ashore without any money. We all would have understood and lent him the money, but he never asked.

He's a tough guy.

He decided to carry on with the race.

We dropped Flash off in Ushuaia, Argentina and he was taken away to the nearest hospital with Ruth and Clive travelling with him.

We needed to get more fuel, food and water and so whilst they were away, we set about the business of getting ready to go back into the Southern Ocean once more.

The fuel pontoon made getting diesel an easy task, some of the team went shopping for food (not me), but we had to wait for a fire tender to come down with a tank full of water later in the day, so we took advantage of the time in various ways.

Most of the crew went into town and had a shower and a meal in a restaurant, then went shopping and 'phoning home.

I stayed with the boat and caught up with some sleep.

We were eating plenty and a shower wasn't really very high on my list of priorities, besides which, there would be food and water to load aboard later and we would be off again as soon as possible.

Now was a good chance for some peace.

Leave me alone.

We got away that evening and were escorted by a pilot boat, via Puerto Williams, back into the Beagle Canal to the Southern Ocean once more.

It was nearly Christmas, our heads were down.

Recent events, including the fact that there were no other boats within 2,000 miles, meant that it was hard to focus on anything outside the boat.

The daily slog of sailing became a routine once more and the watches began to come and go.

All track of days became lost as we thought only about boatspeed and sail trim, then food and sleep.

It was getting hard.

Washing was down to a minimal, the boat was wet through and stank, so did we.

Sleep was a premium and it was hard work physically.

Clive had a few words for us and he posted them on the notice board.

The Team Stelmar plan

The task ahead is a big one, the greatest challenge yet. But I have no doubt at all that this will bring us closer together then ever before and will make us an even greater force to be reckoned with on the race course in future legs.

None of us deserved or expected this; no one can explain the reason or circumstances. As ever things happen in life, I believe for a reason and it is not what happens but how we react and handle it that makes us what we are. We achieved the impossible before and have touched the lives of thousands with our determination and fighting spirit, the only way we know is to continue.

We have to cover the 5,000 miles to Wellington safely and quickly, maintaining our happy boat and close team. We should not underestimate the journey ahead however in this new challenge lie many opportunities; it is the attitude you choose that will affect how we approach it. We will all need new positive goals and objectives.

Along with the resolve that each of you has shown individually we will need strength and determination from each other to endure. No doubt there will be times of frustration and despair for us all, when Wellington will seem further away than ever and when the last place we want to be is where we are, we will all share these emotions. Our strength has been and will be our united approach.

One day New Zealand will appear on the horizon and together we will have achieved something extraordinary. Friends old and new will be united and we will be proud of what we achieved.

Clive Cosby – Skipper Team Stelmar
SAFE, HAPPY, FAST

The words sank in and where we had been resigned, weary and deflated, we now began to look forwards.

At 72 feet long and with Paula's initiative and sense of fun, on December 1st Stelmar became the world's largest advent calendar ... probably.

The bilges, cupboards, bunks, any possible hiding place for chocolate was utilized and became a hiding place. At watch changeover each day at midday, Paula selected an individual to draw a piece of paper out of a plastic bag; the name written on it decided who the smug git was for the day.

The only trouble was you were supposed to find the corresponding "hidey hole" for the day you were given.

For my part, it was a real temptation to play my own game and simply remove any chocolate that I could find, from any hiding place that I could find. I wasn't however, the chocoholic aboard and my upbringing got the better of me.

I wasn't selected until day seventeen and then I couldn't find the blessed hiding place!

In many ways this the most formative period for Team Stelmar.
We began to work together and make an effort to lift our spirits.

We had almost forgotten about the pettiness of the first leg and began to look out for each other.

Things had become a little fractious between Paula and I, despite a good start and when she noticed that I was feeling low one day, she asked if I needed a hug.

I did and she gave me one.

She and I started working together properly.

We all got along much better as we made allowances and compromises.

Most of us were fairly strong characters, but we were learning.

There had been some limits laid down and some personalities began to show through.

Strong and weak.

Team Stelmar began to really take shape.

The offices in London had also been at sixes and fours, as the final negotiations were taking place to sell the company, the repercussions of which were unknown to the yacht crew or London staff.

We felt pretty much alone down there and it looked like we could be without a sponsor too.

David (Chapman) contributed hugely to the positive mood developing when he started writing us a weekly e-mail which was humorous and current and reminded us that we were being watched, supported and loved.

The gloom began to lift.

During a period of absolutely flat calm, Julian initiated the Hazelnut Deck Bowls Championships whilst the Groaners were on watch.

The Jack was a raisin and individuals' hazelnuts were selected from a big bag.

At watch change-over, he handed the mantle to the Grunters as there was still absolutely no wind and we continued the games.

Although we were learning to make allowances with each other, it became obvious once again that we were a competitive bunch, when the boundaries of the rules were explored.

It began with people filing off the point on their nut to help it roll more easily and true. When they began to roll with the roll of the boat in the swell, after you had thought that they had rested and potentially scoring bowls were being dislodged, we began to make the filed edge flat so it would stay put.

It ended up resembling "Shove Hapenny" more than bowls.

I can't remember who won; it seemed to end in a long, protracted SUMO on the rules of Hazelnut Deck Bowling Championships.

I found it enlightening listening to all these experts.

Anyone would have thought that it was a regular sporting event and they were quoting case history.

Once someone suggested performance enhancing drug testing, we moved on.

Phil set up an on-deck gym, we had Yacht Racing Rules forums and discussions, we even considered setting up a Spanish language class.

"Shove, Shag or Marry" was a game whereby an individual is given three celebrity names and they have to decide which one they would shove off a cliff, which one they would shag and by process of elimination, which one they would marry.

The celebrities selected, inevitably would be the most hideous examples of human grotesqueness we could think of.

Hmm!

We were allowed to use the Sat C phone to make a call home either on Christmas Eve or Christmas Day, it was exciting to know that we would be able to spiritually share a small part of Christmas with the people that we loved.

Ruth e-mailed her brother and asked him to mail back with the words of some carols. He did so and on Christmas Eve on the 2200 hrs watch change, we had a carol service on deck.

Better still, we rounded Waypoint Flash on Christmas Eve and began racing once more.

Two thousand miles behind the rest of the fleet, almost certain of a last place finish but beginning to look forward and lift our heads, hoping that we could do enough to get to Wellington before our time limit ran out.

The wind filled Stelmar's sails and we ploughed through the waves with a sense of determination that reflected our new-found optimism.

Daily Log 24th December 2004

Its 0200 hours on Christmas Eve. The wind is howling outside, the rain is tumbling down and the sea state is building.

This Christmas our thoughts are obviously on the job at hand, but if we had time to reflect, there would be so many people that we would like to wish the compliments of the season to in person. Unfortunately there isn't the opportunity to do that, so on behalf of Team Stelmar I would like to pass on our warmest regards and our very best wishes. As we move one step closer to fulfilling our dreams, our thoughts are with our loved ones, may God grant you all peace and happiness this Christmas.

Richard Parson
Team Stelmar - SAFE, HAPPY, FAST

Decorations had been made from various bits of green and red electrical tape and stuck around the galley area, with fifteen chocolates wrapped in silver paper, hung around the ceiling.

Somebody had drawn a tree in green electrical tape on one of the galley cupboard doors and stuck bits of coloured paper on it. The area had taken on a distinct, festive aura.

Christmas Day came with the usual festivities, slightly curtailed, but present nevertheless. Lunch was served at midday with "turkey" and all the trimmings followed by a small ceremony of exchanging presents, mostly some tacky crap hastily purchased in Buenos Aires, but topped up with more during our unexpected visit to Ushuaia.

It was a respite from our world above deck, but the conditions were becoming uncomfortable and quickly we forgot about Christmas and applied ourselves to matters at hand.

Groaner watch went up on deck after lunch and our labours continued.

Christmas wasn't forgotten, but neither was our current, forcefully obvious environment.

The next couple of watches were fairly bland though, due mainly to the fact that it was blowing so hard that there was no need to change any sails, simply keep sailing the boat as fast as we could in the direction of New Zealand, which was a task that fell to the helms.

Work that sea.

We (Paula) could no longer take part in the chat shows between the fleet as we were out of VHF range, so we were a little out of touch with the fleet, other than via e-mail.

On 27th December news started filtering through of a Medivac on Imagine it. Done.

John Masters, a crew volunteer aboard, was seriously ill following an attack of peritonitis. He had fallen heavily in rough seas and that had somehow aggravated his condition.

They were retiring from the leg to get him some help.

There was a great deal of concern about him and it was with great relief that we were to learn that once they were in reach of land, a helicopter had picked him up and he was out of immediate danger.

Apparently they had exhausted their supplies of morphine and had received assistance from two of the other boats, by taking their supplies too.

It was a close call.

John turned out to be okay.

News from the outside world was also scarce and segmented, but information began filtering through of the Tsunami that had devastated Thailand and on New Years Day (midnight on the 31st) we joined the rest of the world in holding a two minute period of silence in memory of all those who perished.

It hugely overshadowed the gravity of our predicament and further helped us to dig deeply within ourselves and push ourselves harder.

The reports from aboard began to take on a lighter feel, but we were still learning to race.

Daily Log 1st January 2004

"The other day" we spotted a whale. It was a huge great thing, by my reckoning longer than our yacht, which is 72' long (as you are probably aware).

If you've ever seen one (a whale that is) you will know that they are truly awesome creatures, especially ones that are that large and that close. When I first spotted it, it was no more than a boat length away from us; the surprise only serving to magnify it's perceived size.

Apparently, when people see a whale for the first time, it is not uncommon to gasp or swear due to the intensity of the feeling. On Team Stelmar, it was the latter. Here is a rough transcript of the whole episode.

*"**!!""** look at the **!!"""** size of that!"*
*"***!!*"*
I quickly rushed to the companionway hatch and shouted to the other watch who were just about to eat lunch.
*"If anyone's interested there's a ***!! Great whale, right beside the boat!"*
Many people rushed up
*"***!!"*
*"!!**!!"*
"!*!"*
We were so occupied in watching this magnificent creature (helmsperson included) that we failed to spot some black clouds sweeping towards us from the opposite direction.

In a flash the wind backed by nearly 180 degrees and increased to 25 knots. We crash tacked and there were a few pairs of wet feet as the whale swam off laughing to itself!

*** !!** Whale!*

Richard Parson
Team Stelmar

I was thinking of our arrival in Wellington though and felt benevolent towards the rest of the crews who were now there and were having a party.

The messages of support that had come from the fleet had been a huge lift and had helped us to stand taller and to be able to look further than our perceived horizon.

Daily Log 4th January 2004

As the leaders sail into Wellington, the celebrations begin. For the first time in weeks, the crews will enjoy fresh food and a few beers as they let their hair down and party in "Windy Wellington."

The daily routines now become more focussed on maintenance and preparing the boats before a thorough examination by the technical team, whilst the crews go off with family and friends to enjoy the sights that Wellington and New Zealand have to offer.

Team Stelmar are still 2,000 miles away, battling through the waves in the never-ending routine of "on watch" and "off watch". Sailing through squalls and rain showers, recording the hourly logs, pressing for more boat speed, changing sails, watching and studying the weather systems, preparing and serving food, cleaning the heads, pumping water out of the bilges and the thousand other things that equate to life aboard.

As we attempt to position ourselves between the next weather systems, gaining every possible advantage that we can from the wind, whilst avoiding the absolute howlers where the wind can exceed 50 knots, our thoughts are with the leaders and the excellent progress that the fleet have made.

After over 6,000 miles of ocean racing, the fleet are separated by only a matter of miles, which is a truly remarkable achievement and a testimony to the professionalism of the skippers and crews.

Whilst they will tell you that their thoughts are with us, I can tell you that our thoughts are with them more! There isn't much I wouldn't give to be where Spirit of Sark, BP Explorer or BG are.

Richard Parson
Team Stelmar

We had experienced our first taste of the Southern Ocean and we still had many miles to cover before reaching New Zealand but we were now looking forward to getting ashore.

We were a pretty weary bunch, the thought of the rest of the fleet arriving was hard to swallow.

We were still cold, wet and uncomfortable and working as hard as we could in order that we arrive in respectable time. It's just that it was getting harder.

Some of the dry-suit seals began to fail, as did the gloves that we were wearing.

As a matter of concern, there was a general recall of all the life-jackets as some non-serious faults were discovered.

Our dry-suits were letting in water from the feet to the seals and it was always cold water that found its way in.

We emptied our boots of cold sea water before we hopped into our bunks.

We slept on wet bunks, with wet socks and base layer clothing and pulled on wet foul weather kit before we went on deck and faced an absolute onslaught of cold.

I was as cold and wet as I have ever been in my life so far.

We were as comfortable as technology will allow, but even that has its limits.

I was reading Sir Ernest Shackleton's book at the time and tried to realise how lucky we were.

We hadn't had it too bad. .

Besides which, we had company as the Vendee yachts sailed the other way.

Daily Log 10th January 2004

Its 2035 hours and we're into the last period in today's Mother watch. Tomorrow, I will be allowed back on deck with the rest of Grunter watch. I've just taken a cup of tea up to "my children" on deck. The wind is a steady 20 knots, the stars are shining and all discussions there are of the Vendee Globe Race and the progress the single-handed sailors are making, some of them are ex-Challenge sailors so needless to say; the race has our full attention and support.

Coming back down the steps towards the galley there seems to be a meeting going on in the foulie locker. It's Wrighty and some of his Merry Men, someone has overfilled the day-tank, resulting in a near diesel spill and there's a "Who Dunnit?" going on. The thing is there is an hourly record kept of who filled it in the ship's log, which is signed, so it's hardly the stuff of Sherlock Holmes. I pass by un-inspired.

What does grab my attention though is Clive. He is sat gazing into the computer screen with a fixed grin on his face. I sidle up to him to investigate. He is considering our arrival and subsequent re-integration into civilised society once we reach dry land after what will be nearly six weeks at sea and has some words of wisdom for us.

The "in-house" jokes, the less than PC humour, the developed table manners and "open and honest" dialogue will have to go, he will be warning us. Climbing over the table once a meal is finished is frowned upon, as is hanging one's laundry on the bed end to dry. It is not a matter of achievement to go for three weeks without washing properly, we will be expected to take the initiative and shower daily, even though we probably won't need to. Furthermore frank discussions on bowel movements are not in the public interest and will soon be frowned upon.

Oh well, it's only for a couple of weeks and then life will return to normal.

We've been through worse.

Richard Parson
Team Stelmar

Although we missed the official arrival party in New Zealand, Flash was there to represent us at the official welcome party.

Because of his standing in the Global Challenge Race Crew Community, he did us proud when he represented Team Stelmar in the official welcoming ceremony.

He was asked to accept the welcome of the fleet from the Maori warrior, by accepting a nose rub. Unfortunately for us and him, it wasn't explained properly.

When Flash whispered to the Maori chief in front of him that he didn't really know what to do, the chief explained,

"We touch noses".

After a moment of shouting and posturing by the warrior, Flash moved forward and touched the warrior's nose with his forefinger.

"No", he said, "We touch each others noses."

Flash moved back to let the warrior touch his nose, thinking that he would then step forward and reciprocate.

"No", he said, "You touch mine and I touch yours!"

By now it was too late, our hero was confused and why shouldn't he be?

"Noses should touch."

"Oh right!"

Back on board, Clive's document was revealed to us.

He had some words of warning as we approached Wellington. We had spent 53 days at sea and our social graces had been allowed to slip.

He had spent quite a lot of time on it, it was obviously meant to be tongue in cheek but there was a serious to it message also.

He posted it on the notice board.

Forum for the Re-integration into Polite Society.

After 50 days at sea we have continued as a strong close team which will stand us in good stead for the future. However, there are some negative effects, which we need to overcome in the remaining days in order to be accepted in New Zealand society, not offend well-wishers and pick-up where we left off with personal relationships!

Let's look at these in more detail

Level of conversation.
It has become commonplace to discuss toilet habits, bowel movements and flatulence. This will soon become unacceptable and we will all have to revert to our polite upbringings, where such matters were strictly taboo and only discussed with somebody of a medical persuasion on a strictly professional basis. We have evolved into a suitably open and honest team, but will need to be less directly honest with outsiders, for example 'that last canapé has gone right through me!' Furthermore it will not be suitable to openly discuss matters of a sexual, personal or private nature in polite mixed company. Outsiders will not be so openly receptive to comments surrounding sexual prowess, technique and preferences; we may also encounter persons of a less favoured sexual persuasion, much more sensitive to such predominantly heterosexual sentiments!

Manners.
Due to the necessary predatory nature and primeval existence adopted onboard, all to a greater or lesser degree have neglected to maintain their

childhood manners. We will all need to continue to remember our Ps and Qs and re-establish a respect for our elders and females present. However my main concern regards table manners; please be warned that I feel table manners in particular, especially eating habits have slipped below publically [sic] acceptable levels. Cutlery should be held correctly and not used to emphasise ones point, comments should be saved and only uttered after mastication is complete. Food should be savoured and enjoyed, even commented on. 'Is there any seconds?' is not the appropriate comment. Much as it has become commonplace to pile up ones crockery and scrape any remaining foodstuffs into one communal bowl before jumping over the table towards the exit, civilised society may require you to curb your actions.

Interpersonal skills.

No longer will it be acceptable to treat other people with contempt, wilfully point out their shortcomings or laugh openly at their human mistakes. Conversations no longer require expletives to provide emphasis, nor should it be commonplace to provoke reaction by antagonising companions. Remember that in jokes will be lost to a wider audience, 'More currants Newton?' will never cease to amuse us, as will wit regarding most peoples inability to pass the day without breaking wind or expressing dislike of being served pasta, porridge or even oatcakes as a meal. However this will all be lost on persons outside of Team Stelmar. They would much rather hear tales of our bravery and heroics on the ocean. But beware a simple curious but intelligent question regarding our escapades does not require a full blow-by-blow account of the last seven weeks. Exaggeration though inevitable may not be appropriate to all audiences. Care should also be taken when recounting tales of life onboard as much nautical terminology does not easily translate to civilian life. Tales of hardening-up, raising your pole and cracking off around a buoy may lessen the general public's perception of us as a wholesome team.

Personal habits.

Trouser trumping or for that matter any voluntary or involuntary orifice utterance will be heavily frowned upon, as will any pride associated with such activity. Further more the hanging of ones laundry from furniture will provoke disapproval from others, where for us it is entirely normal.

For some to be staying in accommodation where a selection of towels is provided will be commonplace for most it will be a luxury and one that we should exploit but not come to expect. Likewise the ability to run the tap for hours, not pump, flush or even clean the heads may be a short lived luxury but one that will be most appreciated. Remember leaving a message in porcelain may not attract the distain of your shipmates whilst ashore, but afloat the opportunity will not be missed to point out your faux pas.

Personal standards.

Showering, shaving and the wearing of clean clothes will soon be expected of us all. No longer will it be a matter of competition to be esteemed as to the length of time one has avoided the shower, not changed ones underwear or even slept in ones foulies. Likewise one should not expect kudos with respect to time taken to dress, drop off the kids, or neglect to brush ones teeth for days on end.

Inter-reaction.

New people will come into our lives; familiar faces will re-appear all expecting our time and efforts. We have become a strong clique, conversation outside of which may at first prove difficult, though ultimately will be necessary. Communication needs to be in a down to earth, polite and sympathetic manner, virtues that most seem to have forgotten. Should it prove to be rewarding and develop beyond introductions and the weather, remember, be careful they are far less likely to be as desperate, practical or as hurried as yourself. They may require an acquaintance period, a thorough assessment of what is in it for them and a level of understanding and emotional re-attachment beyond the moment. You however after a sustained period of abstinence may be looking no further than the Billy Mills Roundabout.*

Following any such activity your chosen partner may be un-amused to hear you relaying the full story to your watch.

Similarly, partners may be un-impressed to discover who we may, during our time of need, have been prepared to lie down next to in a game called "Shove, Shag or Marry".

The Media.

Media opportunities may present themselves, if they do please avoid the desire to burp, fart or similarly express yourself on the PA system. You may amuse yourself even create hysterics amongst your teammates and most loyal of supporters, but beyond this, you will do yourself few favours and guarantee that your only route to the afore mentioned roundabout will be solo.

On a serious note this has been a huge team effort, we did what we had to do and are proud of what the team has achieved. We did this well and have learned a huge amount from it. The way now is forward and the continuing race ahead, we are very grateful for the support received and were touched and inspired by the messages from many. We now need to enjoy these last days together and our well-earned welcome in Wellington before a break from all things nautical. Soon to return invigorated, inspired and invincible.

Fortunately for those that will struggle with compliance you only need do so for three weeks!!

(* The Billy Mill Roundabout is, figuratively speaking, the point of sexual tension immediately before the point of no return. Now read that bit again....)

It was quite a considered piece.

Maybe we really had let go of our personal standards, not that we felt too chastised by it.

J.C. had us sussed;

"....still, corned beef hash, mash potatoes and mushy peas for tea should mean that Phil and Rich will be providing a very base form of entertainment in a couple of hours time!"

John Campbell (aka J.C.)
Extract from the Daily Log 13th January 2005.

When Stelmar did *Rock Up* in Wellington in the middle of the night, there was a lot of noise from the PA system and friends and family. Some alcohol was also consumed both on the pontoons and then later in the local bar.

We were glad to be ashore, we had just had a tough slog.

It was a good feeling to be ashore again.

Newton and JC had been looking forward to "a nice glass of wine" and ought to be singled out here for a special mention but I will spare them their blushes. Suffice to say, David (Chapman) fulfilled some duties not regularly assigned to him.

On their behalf, Thanks David!

Later, they shared a bathroom with each other in the most intimate way, as they hocked their guts up in unison!

Stelmar had arranged for us to stay in a 4 star hotel for the first two nights that we were there, as a surprise *pat on the back*. They were with us completely; the sponsorship was secure with the new owners OSG.

David was there to meet us. He smiled like a demon and we smiled right back at him. He had lived it too.

The hotel surprise added to the feel good factor.

O.S.G. were into Team Stelmar.

Newton and J.C. were sharing a room.

Soul-mates!

The rest of us had a couple of drinks and things began to look up.

Although my hands were shredded I soon forgot them. I was delighted to meet up with some of my closest friends, John Mac and Janet Farrage, who were waiting on the quayside. They had been to Argentina on the last stop-over and had been waiting for me for days in New Zealand.

Great friends, through thick and thin.

A sight for sore eyes.

Tina's flight was due in at the exact time we docked and therefore I was in a quandary as to whether to make my way to the airport and risk passing her on the way, or wait at the bar and hope that she knew where to come to meet me, drinking with John and Janet.

Good sense got the better of me and I stayed put.

It was a good job that I did because in a couple of minutes, a Taxi turned up and delivered my girl.

I heeded Clive's warning about the Billy Mill Roundabout.

Maybe I was getting improved?

The first morning in New Zealand though, we were greeted with an earthquake.

A big chap that woke me up as it happened.

No *Billy*, but no cries of *Geronimo*! either.

The earth moved for all of us.

Awake or asleep.

There was no significant structural damage to the city, but it was alarming.

Maybe it was a sign of the rocky time ahead as it was followed by a further four quakes during the stopover. Apparently they are particularly overdue for a big quake; thankfully there were no major problems whilst we were there.

The whole crew had some time off from the boat, mainly due to the fact that we all worked flat out to get her ready.

As we had arrived on the last day possible before it would have been too late to lift Stelmar out of the water, there was no time to spare. She had to be ready to go back into the Southern Ocean because there would be no time for any major repairs once in Sydney. Don Krafft, a crew volunteer and Navigator aboard Me to You, was waiting for us on the quay. He stayed with us, as did a couple of guys from Save the Children, and helped us with every aspect of the work required, even the shitty stuff in the bilges.

Don particularly, is worthy of a special thank you.

Karen and Adrian were due to come back again for the next leg, together with Nigel Durman and Rona Cant they made up the new team.

Even people that had only intended to sail one leg with us, like Adrian and Karen, were coming back.

I felt quite flattered that we seemed to be working well together and making leggers feel welcome.

Nigel's entrance was the most noteworthy.

He was due in on 30th January, along with the rest of the leggers. There were usually corporate sailing days to staff, as well as re-packing the boat after the clean-up operation of a couple of weeks ago, Challenge events and the Prize giving Ceremonies.

Food had to be packed, bunks to be re-fitted after being cleaned, foul weather kit to be brought back aboard as well as sleeping bags, gas, medical supplies, sails, toiletries... everything really.

It was all used as a familiarization exercise for the leggers and they were expected to arrive on time.

Nigel couldn't manage it, no matter how hard he tried.

And he tried.

Wellington was fog-bound so his arrival flight diverted to Auckland, way up north.

He was kept waiting there, until they could get reports that the fog was lifting and they could fly him and the other passengers down.

Twice they took off from Auckland and then returned to Auckland because Wellington was still fog-bound.

Two days later, Nigel in desperation to arrive, eventually decided to rent a car and drive himself down to us. Unfortunately, as he hit road works near Rotorua, the car in front flung a stone up and it shattered his rented cars' windscreen. He had to wait there while a replacement was driven down.

He arrived three days before race re-start and did none of the work, but enjoyed the best parties.

Nigel had natural style, but shying away from work wasn't his style.

Nobody minded that he was late, we all felt sorry for him.

He missed out a little.

Rona's arrival was also not going to go un-noticed. It had been built up by us all on Grunter Watch to antagonize Paula.

Rona had sailed in the last B.T. Global Challenge aboard Quadstone. Unfortunately for her and for quite a few others, they were involved in a collision just after the start on this leg four years ago, so they were unable to complete it.

Strictly speaking, Rona hadn't sailed all the way around the world yet, but she had only failed on a technicality.

For her it was *unfinished business.*

She had also written a book about her race which, reportedly, was not too complimentary to her crew mates.

It was a widely held (unconfirmed) belief amongst us that Rona would be on our watch and if that was to be the case, she would undoubtedly be in the snake-pit with Paula. We hadn't missed an opportunity to rib Paula, who made no secret of the fact that she wasn't keen on sailing, about the fact that Rona was much more experienced at yacht racing than her and was going to *solve all our problems.*

Needless to say, there were no problems in the snakepit, but inevitably there would be tangles and crises to solve and Paula felt responsible for her position, most of us did.

Considering that she was only going to be on the boat for a week, Rona had a disproportionate effect on Grunter Watch.

Not only weren't our efforts recognized at the prize-giving, there were no official photographers from Challenge Business or On-Edition present when we arrived in port, so no images of us were available to be shown during the evening when the presentation for the leg took place.

I had expected Chay Blyth to acknowledge us in some small way when he addressed the room, maybe even say "Well done."

I was wrong.

We did receive the 24 hour distance record for achieving 259 miles though.

We were getting the Happy and Fast bits.

Just not the complete results that we wanted.

Leg Three – Wellington to Sydney

(Leggers – Karen Smith, Adrian Stafford-Jones, Rona Cant, Nigel Durman)

We had ideas that we could perform better than we had done to date.

Our starting was good, our teamwork was getting better and our boat speed was excellent.

The leggers that we had aboard had all sailed before and there was no real need to bring them up to speed in terms of boat handling and actual sailing. They were also useful below deck and made for a smooth transition from land to sea.

This was a quick, straight line dash in relation to the last two legs with a finish in Sydney, Nicko's home city.

Boat speed was to be critical.

Nicko had sailed quite a lot around there, so we were hopeful that we could get it right this time.

There were two other skippers from Sydney, Matt Riddel on Samsung and Andy Forbes on BG Spirit, so it wasn't a unique advantage, but we hoped it would help.

We were still smiling from winning the fastest boat over a twenty four hour period on the first leg.

We knew we could be quick.

Also, we had something to prove after the mishaps of the last leg.

In light winds, we were the first boat off the start line.

As the fleet got started, the wind filled in.

We rounded a couple of laid marks, hoisted our spinnakers and led the charge towards the Tasman Sea and Sydney.

We were off, although before we got out of Wellington Harbour, Samsung overtook us to windward whilst we sailed downwind with our kites up and with land obstructing the way ahead of them, effectively blocking any way through. We should have defended our position but we let them through.

Maybe I should have taken a more magnanimous approach, after all, we had quite a few miles ahead of us. We continued to sail lower than the rest of the fleet and as they began to harden up on to the wind, they got an advantage over us and as we came out of Wellington Harbour, we emerged in the middle of the fleet.

Being involved with the rules, I would be critical about the situation today if you were to ask me about it in the privacy of a public bar after a couple of glasses of Guinness.

There were only fifteen to twenty knots of breeze; we were probably only sailing at a boatspeed of around eight knots.

Closure between yachts was not exactly lightning pace.

We could easily have shut the door on them.

We let them through.

I wrote the first log on this leg.

Daily Log 6th February 2005

At 1430 hours (local time) on Sunday 6th February, the Challenge fleet restarted the 2004/5 Global Challenge Yacht Race from Wellington, New Zealand.

The wind was blowing around 20 knots from the north and the sun was shining. The conditions were idyllic as the fleet first rounded a couple of laid marks in Wellington Harbour, then hoisted their promotional spinnakers before heading off towards Cook Strait between North and South Island, according to one local, on our way to the West Island!

After all the problems of the last leg, Stelmar led the pack away from the start to the absolute delight of our crew and supporters. Nothing could have been more effective at brightening our day.

During the first twenty-four hours there are bound to be plenty of place changes as we escape the gusting influence of the land and the tidal rips, once at sea we can settle down to what promises to be a real nail biter of a race.

Nothing can be certain until the finishing gun sounds in Sydney Harbour. This time however, we would like to be catching some of the other boats' mooring lines as they arrive.

Richard Parson
Team Stelmar – Safe, Happy, Fast.

We kept *'scratching away'* (Clive's oft repeated phrase) at the rest of the fleet and on Monday, when the wind had dropped slightly to between 10-12 knots, there were ten other yachts in sight.

We were in the middle of the pack, powered up, with the bit between our teeth, making great boatspeed and catching the leaders.

C'mon Stelmar!

As the night fell it all came to a pathetic halt and the wind dropped right away to between 2-4 knots and we slowed to a snails pace.

There was good news in the six hourly sked though, we were up into third place.

Spirits were lifted and life aboard took on the routine of sail trim, boat-speed, eat, sleep, sail trim, boatspeed …

The weather was mild and the watches during the day were a pleasant experience. At night the skies were so clear and the stars so abundant that it was a staggering sight.

Phosphorescence sparkled in the water, we saw satellites and shooting stars galore, sharks and whales in the first few days, as well as thousands of Bluebottle jellyfish.

Dolphins were no longer really counting as a special siting.

It was a magical time.

It was great to be at sea again, although the fact that many of the other boats were regularly in view, served as a constant reminder to continue to keep the pressure on the others by making the boat go as quickly as we could and not to dwell on all that was around us.

Well, we were to keep an eye on the boats around us, obviously. Not Just the phosphorescence and stars, but the shooting stars and wildlife too.

Not that we had been going soft on that.

This was a short leg and was going to go to the wire.

We needed to stay focused.

The wristwatch alarm, which was attached to the frame around the wheel, was still pinging every fifteen minutes, to remind us to log our performance on the laminated sheets stuck up on deck. We were all involved in monitoring it and concentrate on every aspect of boat speed from sail trim, to the course steered by the helmsmen and woman.

As well as by day, sail trim at night was constant,

We had some pretty powerful torches aboard and we aimed for better all the time.

Leading the charge on the keenness front for the most powerful handheld torch ever, was Phil.

He practically went on a one man mission to ensure that we had effective, working, powerful torches of all kinds, for all occasions.

He re-wired, re-designed and re-built all the handheld ones, including personal ones, time and time again.

He even gave some of them names like 'The Twins' and 'Big Yellow'.

Big Yellow was a one million candle power chap.

He was pretty much as good as you get in term of torches.

Most of the bow teams had now started wearing (nameless) head torches when working up at the front. For close stuff like sail changes or peels, it meant that you could work hands free, although there is a certain amount of thought that has to go into their usage. It's easy to look straight at someone when you are talking to them and instantly blind them for the next five minutes.

Something you wouldn't be thanked for ... obviously.

The wind, when it came back on Wednesday night/ Thursday morning, had plenty of east in it which allowed us to sail using our spinnakers, or at least sail at a broad reach.

It meant that speeds were great and life was relatively stable aboard with living conditions below deck as comfortable as they get.

As Thursday morning became lunchtime, we could clearly see both Spirit of Sark and Samsung. The three O'clock sked placed us officially third, with Samsung and Sark slightly ahead, we could see them and we were close.

Trim, trim, trim.

By 2100 hours, we were officially in the lead with slightly over a mile between us and the second placed boat.

On Thursday night the wind picked up to thirty knots, gusting to a peak at thirty-nine knots, (Gale Force according to the Beaufort Scale.) so the flanker was dropped in favour of the headsails and the race for the finish began.

The conditions were then ideal for us.

There was still plenty of water coming over the bow and occasionally sweeping down the decks and damping down all the crew.

One of the problems that we were experiencing was the hydro-static valves on the life-jackets. As the jackets kept getting soaked, the gas canister kept going off and automatically inflating our jackets.

They were even going off in the foulie locker because the atmosphere in there was so damp. Well, Newton's kept going off in there.

In the end we removed them and relied on the hope that we could manually inflate them if we needed to.

We only had a couple of dozen spare canisters so the best thing to do was to clip on and not rely on your life-jacket.

We were barreling along at pretty much maximum boatspeed, in the exact direction that we wanted to go. For now, there was very little opportunity for other boats to pass us, other than direct boatspeed and we were getting good at that.

We did have some choices to make though. As we approached the Australian coast, we would have to tackle the East Australian Current, which winds around in a clockwise direction off the east coast. The problem bit was on the approach to Sydney. It was running east, against us.

There was also an area of high pressure opening up and the winds were forecast to go light once more. Get it wrong and you could really suffer.

All of a sudden the race was going to open wide, for anyone to take.

We wanted to win so badly, that it sometimes distracted us and we had to remind ourselves to keep pushing.

There were whispers about how good it would be when we came in first.

BG Spirit headed way up north to try and avoid the worst of the current and to try and find a little more wind up there. Most of the rest of the fleet went to the south of the flow, whilst Sark, Samsung and Stelmar ran through the middle.

It didn't work for us.

The wind dropped off and we found ourselves running against a four knot current at times. BG sped home and cracked open the champagne.

We sailed through Sydney Heads in the morning sunshine on Sunday 13th February closely followed by Samsung and yapping at the heels of Spirit of Sark.

Once we cleared the Heads, we were all due to radio Challenge Race Office and give them notice of our approximate finishing time.

We clearly heard Sark, who were just ahead of us, inform Challenge via their VHF radio, that their ETA was one hour.

Julian was our radio operator and was already carrying one of the hand-held radios, all suitably charged.

As quick as a flash, he radioed Challenge race office. He knew well that the crew aboard Sark would be able to hear us, just as we had heard them;

'Challenge race office,
Challenge race office,
Challenge race office
This is Challenge Forty Three, Team Stelmar,
Our estimated time of arrival is fifty-nine minutes!'

We were still smiling.

The finish was right up near Darling Harbour and as we sailed up towards the Harbour Bridge and the Opera House, a couple of launches came out to meet us. They had been chartered by family and friends (organised by Vale) and had come to welcome us in.

They were under strict instructions to wear their Stelmar T-shirts and not to shout to us, as we were still racing.

There were to be no interruptions until we had finished.

I felt that it was inevitable that we would look over and wave, maybe they should have just come to the finish line rather than intercept us, if it was so off-putting.

After eight days at sea, we finished on Sunday 13th February and headed straight for Darling Harbour and a beer.

More protests

At a hearing held on 15th February, the protest brought against Vaio by Unisys – Imagine it. Done. was upheld by the International Jury. It was found that Rule 10 (Port & Starboard) had been infringed at the second mark (Ngaurang Mark) in Wellington Harbour and, in accordance with SI 9.1. three points would be deducted. This dropping them from joint 5th place to 7th.

At a separate hearing, Pindar were awarded a 2-point penalty for losing their 2.2oz spinnaker on leg 2. This, according to the Sailing Instructions whereby a yacht that loses a sail, or damages it in a way to be considered by the race committee to be *Beyond Economical Repair*, shall receive an appropriate penalty.

At the prize-giving ceremony there were no photos of our arrival on the evenings projected slideshow of photos taken during the last we didn't get a *Well Done!* from Chay or any of the other Challenge staff on the rostrum, but Team Stelmar weren't without mention.

We enjoyed our moment of glory when we picked up the prize from Pindar for being the first boat off the start line in B.A. and the Challenge 24 hour run record for covering the most miles in a 24 hour period.

Two more prizes to add to the tally.

Leg Four – Sydney to Cape Town

(Leggers – Sarah Powis, James Smith, Rob Buchan & Ben Pike)

This time, we didn't know any of the leggers, however, I am now of the opinion that God sent Ben Pike as a personal test to Richard Parson.

The current team were settled nicely into Sydney.

Paula had volunteered to go the airport to meet our additional crew, welcome them in and to bring them back to their accommodation when the time was right.

Sure enough, she turned up, held aloft a Stelmar banner, stood with the BG Group Welcome Party so as to associate herself with the Global Challenge Race and waited at arrivals.

They had been told to look out for someone.

None of this lot saw her and her whacking great banner!

The first to turn up and come straight to the apartment that I was sharing with Tigger and Phil was Ben Pike.

'Pikey'.

Far from being bashful, he launched into a full on tirade about his view on everything and everyone. He was pretty cock-sure, although apart from the bare minimum Challenge training programme, he'd never been sailing before.

He had an opinion on everything, but from a yacht racing point of view he knew Jack.

First impressions count, I think that's a lesson the boy could still learn.

He didn't really exceed anyone's expectations as far as I'm aware, least of all mine.

Next in were Sarah and James.

Sarah had met some of the BG Group welcome party and had got so locked into conversation with a couple of BG leggers that she had been talking to on the flight, that she had walked right past Paula and had shared a cab with the BG guys.

I can tell you on good authority that she still carries their merchandise on a daily basis and not Stelmar's.

Also she turned up with a pillow, the same as Newton had done.

That augured well!

She used the same explanation as to why she needed it, when no-one else did, as Newton had done many months before.

Kate homed in on her immediately and further explained what she would be allowed to bring along with her and more importantly, what she wouldn't.

All the leggers had received their lists and instructions as to what they were allowed to bring and what they were not, it was anything but ambiguous but some people translated it differently than others.

We actually weighed our stuff.

Some of them didn't seem to give a damn.

The second pillow came.

That'll be due to a precedent then.

Goodness only knows what Kate had diverted though, on this occasion and many others.

James seemed more down to earth.

He was positive, enthusiastic and fit in immediately with the three of us. Admittedly all three were from Grunter watch and all took a pretty basic enjoyment out of life.

He seemed nervous, yet eager and keen to be a part of the team.

Admittedly we didn't represent the entire crew, but he wanted to fit in and take part right away.

He seemed like a top bloke.

He wasn't too experienced in yacht or dinghy racing, neither was Rob Buchan who made his own way there.

I met Rob the following day.

He was immediately interested in maintaining the winches, amongst other things.

He came on to our watch.

Phil and I named him *'The Apprentice.'*

He fitted in with the pair of us straight away and later, *The Apprentice* became our *Fearless Number Three.*

There was another legger of interest though. This one was sailing aboard Pindar.

His name was Nigel Cosby.

Clive's younger brother.

Now it was personal.

Leg Four started on Sunday 27th February 2005

As usual, the twelve yachts jockeyed for position in the thirty minutes from the first time signal which was given at 1330 hours by the race committee. The usual ten-minute warning gun was followed by the five-minute preparation signal and the starting gun was fired at 1400 hours.

Team Stelmar led the fleet for the third start.

On that grey afternoon, the fleet sailed towards Sydney Heads in between 12 – 20 knots of breeze and headed towards the infamous Southern Ocean for the second time.

The forecast that we had been given predicted favourable breezes of between 15-20 knots for the first couple of days, followed by a ball-busting squall by the time we got to the Bass Strait. Not really the news that we had been hoping for. (The Bass Strait carries a similar reputation to that of Cape Horn. Another area of the world that sailors dread, for its tumultuous seas and raging gales.)

We were the first boat over the line and spirits soared. By the time that we had reached Sydney Heads, BP Explorer had overtaken us and our heads went down.

Grunter watch were relieved to grab an hours sleep, whilst Groaner watch took up the mantle. The wind dropped away to between 6 – 10 knots and the rest of the fleet slowly overtook us.

Overnight, in the relatively still airs, we tacked Stelmar a dozen times each time losing momentum and distance. We sailed ourselves to the back of the fleet.

It wasn't until 1500 hours (local time) on Monday when the wind had picked up to around 20 knots from a more northerly direction and we had changed down from the race kite to the flanker that we drew equal 12th place with Samsung.

Barclays Explorer, who were next to us last night and had resisted the temptation to keep tacking, had taken twenty-five miles out of us and were now in 3rd place.

By Tuesday 1st March, the wind was blowing from the north at between 18 – 26 knots, the sun was shining and we were barreling along with the flanker up and the race kite on deck ready for a predicted easing of wind strength. We made a maximum of just over 16 knots boat speed in those conditions, things began to look up.

It's impossible to do anything other than smile and feel positive when you're helming in those conditions.

They are the very best.

The forecast though, had predicted the wind to go more to the west and there was a low-pressure system of 944 mb hanging around ominously near the Bass Strait, which could mean some seriously strong winds and big seas. When I came off watch at 1200 noon (local) I folded up my foul weather jacket and trousers and together with my sunhat, stowed them behind one of the Curver boxes used for containing our personal kit. I replaced them with my drysuit and thermal hat.

Things were beginning to get colder and there was likely to be our first real blow of this leg in the next few hours.

In the hours leading up to the 1720 hours wake-up call, I dreamed of oversized bulls running amok inside an undersized china shop and the torment of our possible encounter with the Bass Strait, all the time waiting for the inevitable crashing, smashing, pitching and rolling that goes on below deck when the wind blows.

The constant damp, the foul smells, the extreme effort required to do anything, both above and below deck, the physical shredding and the mental anguish were playing hard on my mind.

When Grunter watch did come on deck, we spent the dark hours watching some spectacular lightning displays in the distance and awaited the inevitable.

The wind continued to blow and the waves grew bigger. The fleet sked that we received from race office that evening showed us having covered 65.5 miles in the last six hours, which was the fleet's top run and we had moved up into eleventh place.

One down, ten to go.

"Keep Scratching!"

We were spared the worst of the weather at the Bass Strait. The low pressure system moved away and whilst we had 40 knots, it wasn't anywhere near as bad as my dream.

The new crew had to find their feet.

Pikey and Jim were placed on Groaner Watch whilst Sarah and *The Apprentice* joined us on Grunter watch.

Ben had took a tumble in the first couple of days as the boat pitched in the swell and had banged his head hard enough for Kate and Paula to be concerned about him and brought him below to put him in his bunk.

They were checking for concussion and asked him things like what day it was, or what time it was, but he didn't know.

In itself, that is not unusual because you tend to live by watches and not days but he seemed unable to answer any questions.

When they decided on asking him his name, he tried to be clever by reversing the letters and said "Neb".

They asked him a couple of times but he wouldn't be serious. They decided that he must be okay and left him in his bunk, deciding to check him every half an hour.

I didn't say anything, but I was niggled by his manner.

I guess I could have been taking things too seriously, but he had already irritated me and nothing that I saw ingratiated him.

The last time was when we were all called on deck on start day, but Sue and Ben were missing and I was sent below to find them.

They were sat at the computer and I told them that they were wanted on deck. He wanted to look at the computer and felt that I was interrupting them, or more importantly, him.

He brought that up a couple of times.

Once I had seen his array of cameras and spent some time with him, I decided to keep as far away from him as I could.

He also refused to swap sides (hot bunk) like everybody else on the boat was doing and I realized that if he and I were going to both make it to Cape Town, I had better avoid him.

We struck it lucky with Rob and Sarah though. Rob was well used to the cold and damp conditions, so just kept soldiering on and Sarah was a fairly competent sailor who was particularly good at trimming the mainsail.

As well as the pillow, Sarah brought a positive attitude and an infectious smile to the team.

The other thing that new crew needed a bit more guidance on, was the food preparation times and dilution rates.

Although Ruth had spent a lot of time writing, printing and laminating the crew cook-book, we had developed it since its conception many months ago and no longer necessarily followed it to the letter.

As we got to know how we preferred different meals, we adapted their preparations.

We forgot to tell the leggers.

Some of their early efforts left a lot to be desired.

Our fault really, later we learned to have someone run through things with them on their first couple of times on Mother, rather than just wait to see what they offered us and then rip their heads off.

"Good plan boys!"

There was more upset from Sue who was still whittering away about the daily logs.

She wrote some logs occasionally and wanted to write more.

She was a nuisance at times. As I remember it, more times than not.

I had been taking the photos and video at the start and finish of the legs to date, due mainly to my interest and activity on the team website. I was also involved in discussing and advising the helm and Clive or Nicko on the technicalities of the yacht racing rules. (Wrighty, Alex, Phil and others, that could help with the rules, had other jobs to deal with.) As a practical result of these two jobs, I would perch myself on the frame behind the helmsman so that we could talk to each other whilst I filmed and snapped away.

Clive had asked Sue to take the photos and video for the start of this leg, whilst I went up on to the bow to work with Phil.

I'd have to raise my voice to be heard.

I could do that!

Anyway, Sue had taken the photos at the start, as requested and had transferred them on to the boat media computer, now that she had figured out how to do that.

Later, I selected three, of the ten or so taken and sent them in to Challenge for use on their website.

Sue felt that I had made a poor choice and had let her down. (She was still to grasp the team ethos, everything was personal for her.) Maybe I could have selected a better one, but she inferred that it was vindictive on my part and immediately complained to Wrighty and Clive.

I wasn't being vindictive or gamely and the situation was becoming tiresome.

I apologized to Sue and asked her if she would like to choose the next few photos to be sent in and, by way of going that extra mile, I offered to let her do my next log, thereby doing three in a row and choosing the photos to be sent.

I then had a quiet word with Paula and asked her if she would like to pick up as *Media Officer* for Grunter watch.

I would continue with the responsibility of keeping our own team website up to date, but wouldn't have to really get involved with the daily logs. I would spend less time with Sue more time on deck as a result.

I was better off, but from a media point of view, the team wasn't.

Paula already had a big input in other aspects of the media side of things and had had a couple of reports published in the national press back at home, via a contact that she had at the Daily Telegraph and she regularly hosted the inter-fleet *Chat Shows* over the radio.

She knew what was going on in the rest of the fleet and was popular.

She agreed to take it up, but would get others involved in helping to write logs.

She didn't want to take it over, Sue could wear that little badge.

Paula really did me a favour that day.

I had a word with Clive and told him of my thoughts.

He said that he was sorry and slightly disappointed, but let me do it.

Sue started working closely with Ben Pike.

I was glad to be able to spend more time on deck.

By Thursday 3rd March, I was pretty happy with my lot. We left the coast of Tasmania to starboard and headed for the Southern Ocean once more.

The wind picked up to thirty knots by lunchtime and was forecast to continue for the next twelve hours.

During the 1800-2200 hrs watch, we were on deck and I was helming nearly all of the time.

The wind was fresh, blowing at around thirty knots, and the seas and the boat were in lively spirits.

At watch change-over, we had adopted a *'one up, one down'* policy. Today, when Wrighty noticed a distinct lack of movement at the watch change over, he called out to ask why it had stopped.

The reply came from Phil below deck, who was on Mother;

'No-one wants to come up!'

The Southern Ocean was beginning to stamp it's authority on us.

News came filtering through, from one of Paula's numerous, in fact complete list of contacts throughout the rest of the fleet, about a Medivac from Kids (Save the Children).

It was getting harder for all of us.

Information was scarce but it seemed that they had someone in trouble and had to turn back for help.

Even though we didn't know what the trouble was, we knew what they were going through as a team and as individuals.

It was disappointing and called for a certain amount of soul searching.

They had been really supportive of us as a team in the early stages of the race when we had been through our ordeal, we felt closer to them than anyone in the fleet.

We felt for them.

We plodded on, but that night we had one of the toughest sail changes to date.

The call was made to change up from the storm staysail to the staysail in thirty-two knots of wind. The predicted wind was much lighter and the idea was to get maximum sail up early, so that we could take full advantage of the reducing breeze and maybe get an advantage.

It seemed too early a change for the bow team going forwards.

Alex took the wheel and in winds gusting up to thirty-seven knots, we wrestled with our duties on the bow.

Before going up we would always gather together as a team and talk through what we were going to do. Once we had completed the task, we would discuss it once again to see whether we could iron out any difficulties that may have arisen.

It was good practice, we felt and we held it in high regard.

We were getting bounced around so much by the waves that Alex actually tacked the boat through three hundred and sixty degrees whilst we were up there.

There was water everywhere, we were clipped on but with the waves and the spray washing us and the sails around the foredeck, being hardly able to see, together with the noise of the wind and the shouting, made it pretty extreme.

Phil was on Mother which meant that I was running the bow. I had *The Apprentice* as my Number Two, Sarah as my Number Three and Newton as my Number Four.

The two leggers and Newton!

We had our work cut out, but we did it.

Well done guys.

Sorry for shouting!

It was also getting colder as we headed south, towards the freezer.

Occasionally, whilst working on the front, we would suffer from *Ice Cream Headaches*.

So called, because of the throbbing that most of us could remember feeling as children, as a result of eating too much ice cream, too quickly and suffering a deep headache as a result.

The water was just as cold as that ice cream, as were the wind and the rain and we were feeling it.

We all had the same clothing but there was a new idea to keep warm that some of the crew adopted. Blowing some air into our dry-suits acted as an extra layer of insulation and Michelin men and women started appearing all over the boat, as if by magic. I didn't follow suit because I felt constricted by wearing a balloon but it seemed to work for those that tried it.

Outside conditions completely ruled our lives.

It seemed that from the heat of the tropics, to the cold of the south and everything in between, there were inherent problems.

I was pre-occupied by the fact that my hands were in a sorry state. They were never in good condition, but the harsh conditions played havoc and the skin kept on peeling and splitting, making them extremely tender and sore.

I still carry some small scars from simple splits today.

The diver's gloves that we all wore were excellent kit but they became pretty rancid after a few weeks of wearing them and the insides stank to high heaven. They could be rinsed out but seemed impossible to dry.

Warm, damp conditions were an ideal breeding environment for bacteria and cocooned inside these health hazards were bleeding raw hands.

No wonder they weren't getting any better.

We all suffered various skin complaints and bumps, cuts and bruises but there was very little that could be done to remedy the situation, just grin and bear it.

And don't smell the inside of your gloves ... obviously.

By the 11th March, we had spent three days with wind-speeds consistently exceeding thirty knots on the nose and we were exhausted, grabbing any sleep was nearly impossible.

We had two gusts over fifty knots that night, but as well as the discomfort; we saw the magical sight of the Aurora Australis (the Southern Lights).

The shimmering cloud of illuminated dust appeared like a curtain drawing across the Southern skies. Slowly getting bigger and more spectacular as the night drew on.

It was absolutely spell-binding, like seeing an apparition or a ghost.

They appeared regularly over the next three nights.

Fantastic.

The wind whistled through the rigging, big waves piled up and sometimes caught us by surprise.

Team Stelmar took a bit of a beating.

We were tossed around both on deck and below and there were a few bumps and bruises.

We had put some webbing around the guard-rails on the bow to keep sails and crew from slipping between them. The resulting extra resistance against the breaking waves meant that we broke four of the stainless steel stanchions on the bow in a couple of days and it was then two days before the sea state was reduced enough for it to be safe to send someone onto the bow to replace them.

Sue tripped and lost her balance and got splashed by one of the waves frequently breaking over the boat. In re-counting the tale, a HUGE freak wave was named as the culprit.

It always tickled me to hear people describing it as the work of 'Freak Waves'.

Anything that caused us bother, whether it was something getting broken, a drenching, a violent roll of the boat, or washing things along the deck, it was described as the work of a *Freak*.

All I could think of was that there were obviously more freaks than non-freaks.

I had hardly seen any.

To me, they are rarer than seeing a sperm whale and they are massive.

What makes it a '*Freak Wave*' anyway?

Maybe I had hold of the wrong end of the stick when thinking that it was about the wave.

Perhaps it was so-called because of who it was intended for?

We hit fifty-six degrees south overnight on the 12th and turned north again in snow, hail and rain.

Big waves jumped up at us through the black night and seemed to appear out of nowhere. Mostly though, we could hear the rolling crash above the noise of the wind screaming in the rigging, as waves got near.

Sometimes they would appear really close by, coming at us from all angles.

Sometimes we bobbed over the top of them, sometimes they came down on us, hardly giving enough time to shout a warning, sometimes we fell off the back of them.

We were struggling.

It was rough.

Everyone had to look out, but it was usually the helm that shouted as they were looking forward.

We were really pushing now.

The *boot* (waterproof seal) at the deck mast step got washed away and water came pouring through the resulting gap in the deck, at the base of the mast.

First class got disturbed.

Paula and Newton pumped the water out of the bilges like crazy, whilst Phil and I made a repair at the mast.

We received an *Ice Cream Headache* apiece but we fixed the leak and First Class were able to sleep in their for'ard compartments.

For safety, when we were reefed right down to the minimum amount of sail and we simply had to keep the boat sailing along the given course, we reduced the amount of crew on deck to three during these conditions.

One helming, one riding shotgun and one on the mainsheet.

The rest of the watch were ready to come up if required, but otherwise we could hang on in the relatively comfortable conditions below and eat chocolate or hold a warm mug in our hands.

The shotgun and mainsheet guys spent just a half an hour on deck, whilst the helms spent three-quarters of an hour before being relieved.

The boat was getting bounced around all over the place and occasionally Clive or Nicko would poke their heads up and say "Come up two degrees."

It was all that we could do to keep the boat moving forwards and on more than one occasion, we tacked through three-hundred-and-sixty degrees after having been knocked off course whilst in the process of trying to cope with conditions.

To be told that you were just two degrees off course was seen more as an achievement than a rebuke.

If only we could just be a couple of degrees off, that would be fine, I was aiming for anywhere in a fifteen degree arc!

People inevitably found life tough on deck but some people seemed to simply go on deck, sit in the relative comfort of the cockpit and bunker down for a half an hour before going back down below again to their chocolate.

The cockpit person was supposed to be alert and ready to ease the mainsheet during the bigger gusts and pull it in again afterwards.

During a watch change-over, I was helming waiting for my replacement to come on deck. Pikey came up and bunkered down, I shouted to him to come back to the mainsheet but he wouldn't.

I *'required him'* to.

He didn't.

No further endearment there then.

Daily log 19th March

So, there's this thing. "They" (that is the people that talk about this kind of thing) call it "The Comfort Zone".
It's a bit of a parody really, describing it, it sounds like a child's riddle.

You can feel it, but you can't touch it. You can move it's boundaries, but you can't see it. We all own one, but they are all differing sizes with differing limits. You can live inside it, but it offers no real protection from the elements.

Imagine the first time that you rode a bicycle without stabilisers. At the time, it felt like a huge step forward. Scary, yet exciting. That's the limit of your comfort zone and by the time you have fallen off your bike a few times, you begin to get the hang of it. Your limit moves and before you know it, you are pulling "wheelies" and riding with "no hands".

Okay, now imagine four years of training for this race. Gales galore, sail changes, reefs, qualifications, miles under the belt etc. etc.

Now take off the stabilizers.

After nearly five thousands miles sailing in the Southern Seas, I'm not ready to do "no hands" yet!

This is seat of the pants stuff; I didn't know I had a comfort zone before, now I don't know how far I can stretch it. But stretch it I am, massively.

Richard Parson
Team Stelmar – Safe, Happy, Fast.

Conditions stayed 'bouncy' for the next few days, life aboard followed the same routine.

It seemed that during the rougher weather, a disproportionate amount of time was needed at the nav station from Nicko and Clive.

We only saw them occasionally, usually if they came rushing up on deck, it meant that they had seen the latest sked and it was poor.

They would then run us ragged and make some appalling decisions, which would unsettle everyone.

On 19th March, Clive took on the appearance of someone who had received a bad sked and rushed up on deck in a dither.

He called for an immediate tack, so everyone grabbed the position nearest to us, to enable the manouevre to happen promptly.

Ruth was sat at the back of the boat as usual and was next to the Yankee winch.

It meant that she would have to use some muscle power and grunt.

The only trouble was, she wasn't really that sort of person and therefore, during the tack, the new working sheet was left to flog.

The resulting tangle has got to be one of the biggest knots in a sheet that I have ever seen.

We eventually had to tack back, remove the tangle and take it down below to untangle it. We also altered the sheeting angle on the sail as we re-tied the new sheet, so when the opposite watch changed the headsail down the following day, we broke the leech-line.

Down came the sail and below decks it went for repair.

We sailed without a Yankee for the next twenty-four hours.

Hmm!

We rounded Waypoint Bravo on 23rd March in the early hours of the morning and later that day were surprised at the wildlife that some of us thought that they saw.

During the afternoon, a few dozen pilot whales swam alongside us for at least three quarters of an hour and we were slightly distracted by them.

Almost like dolphins, but bigger and slower in the water.

We all saw them.

Later, Sue swore blind that she saw a swan. We were miles from anywhere. Obviously nobody else saw it.

The other oddity was an Easter Bunny making an appearance and clutches of chocolate eggs started appearing in hiding places all over the boat.

Paula had organised it and had even brought a Bunny outfit.

It was announced on the daily VHF radio *chat show* conversations amongst the fleet.

There was obvious interest for some photos.

She looked good, but we sent them pictures of Tigger in the same kit.

Tee! Hee!

Better than my backside, I suppose.

That is what I remember most about the Easter but it is not what I'm most remembered for reportedly.

Our Easter Bunny (Paula, not Tigger) had organised an Easter Egg Hunt.

Eggs were semi-hidden all over the boat and whoever found them was their rightful owner.

Finders keepers.

We all liked chocolate and everyone was vigilant.

I found the first clutch of half a dozen eggs though and I scoffed the lot.

There was some suggestion that I could have shared them.

They were only little chaps and if I'd kept one and shared five, which of my watch mates should I leave out?

What I'm remembered most for though was my reaction to finding some in my bunk.

Some eggs had been hidden on my bunk and I had not noticed them. We were hot bunking and at watch change-over my opposite number hadn't noticed them either.

We had both slept on them once and then I had slept on them again. They had melted and gone over my bunk, sleeping bag and clothes, I resist saying *all over* my kit, as I mentioned they were only little chaps.

Nevertheless, I grumbled to anyone in earshot that I wasn't impressed and would appreciate it if people refrained from making a mess on my stuff.

Not quite the spirit I agree.

BRING ME THE HEAD OF THE EASTER BUNNY!

We had some real concerns as well, one of which was the battens in the mainsail and their luff boxes, where they were fixed in place.

One of the battens had worked its way out of the luff box which holds it in place and although it wasn't critical to the sail shape, it was in danger of getting worse and could possibly put a hole in the mainsail.

On the 24th, Wrighty spent two hours up the mast trying to fix it. Less than twenty minutes after he came down, it popped out again.

The following day Phil had a go.

Ditto.

Sometimes, if jobs couldn't be completed in a predicted time scale or the predicted time-scale meant that one person couldn't stay awake that long, they were handed over to the following watch.

Nobody was a clock-watcher but if there were dozens of hours of work still to be completed, it made sense to hand over, rather than stick it out and the finish of the job out of obstinacy.

Somebody else could have done a better job because they were alert.

Best for boat, eh?

We took a pride in any jobs that we undertook, mostly and were keen to see them through.

Sometimes we needed help or advice but we didn't easily hand jobs over, or resolve responsibility for something that we had started.

It was too bouncy to be messing around anywhere, especially up the rig, but we needed peace of mind.

Things were rubbing up there in the stretches and strains that were inevitable.

We needed to make sure that nothing was wearing through.

The daily deck safety checks were completed by Julian and Newton.

The rig checks by someone else.

Usually Phil, Alex, Flash or Wrighty.

Unfortunately, the rig checks couldn't always be completed daily as the roll of the boat is magnified as you climbed further away from the centre of gravity and climbing the rig is always treacherous.

It was bad enough on deck.

When Kate took a tumble on deck and emerged with a dented head, obviously concussed, she spent the next four days being Mother, with regular checks on her, including waking her every 20 minutes or so to ask her questions when she was off watch.

A pretty treacherous way to make a diagnosis really, if you think about it.

The days just merged into one another, especially with that kind of irregular sleep pattern.

Watches and boatspeed were what we thought about.

You were either on for one or two 4 hour watches at night and you were either on for the 6 hour morning watch or the 6 hour afternoon watch.

We should have asked her crew number, the sail plan flying when she was last on deck or our position at the latest sked, not what day it was or what date it was.

The decks were often awash and one day when another wave came crashing down over the deck, Newton who was just coming up from below deck, was closing the hatch and was facing forward.

He got a thorough soaking.

I was helming and therefore looking forwards.

I saw it at the last minute and from behind my hood and collar, having no time to yell, I smiled to myself.

As the decks cleared, it became obvious that Paula had clocked me, by seeing my eyes give away a smile.

She glared at me sternly and declared, 'You're supposed to shout *Look out!* Not laugh!'

It couldn't have happened to a nicer guy.

Tee! Hee!

I was due to be Mother on 31st March, so started the day with me in a foul mood, as was usual for me on Mother.

The wind was picking up and I would far rather have been on deck. Fortunately for me, but less so for Rob, he had put his back out and asked if he could be Mother to allow him the chance to rest it.

It meant that I was allowed back on deck with the others for the 1200 – 1800 hours watch.

We put in six sail changes and two reefs as the wind ranged from 10 – 35 knots.

We had more of the same on the 2200 – 0200 hours watch and Groaner watch had the same from 0200 – 0600 hours.

'Remember', Clive said (quoting Flash), 'Pain is temporary, Pride is forever.'

We were run ragged.

Spirits were high though and we were up for the task.

Phil and Pikey wrote the daily log for the 1st April. They doctored a photograph of Stelmar and some of our crew pointing towards an imaginary object at sea.

The object which they inserted into the photograph resembled a submarine's periscope and the log was an April Fool's Day prank about us receiving some assistance from an Australian submarine.

They wrote that the submarine had been tracking the Challenge fleet and had noticed us slowing up. Upon investigation (underwater, obviously) they noticed that we had snagged a net and they had freed it, thus accounting for our erratic boat speeds.

Daily log 1st April - April Fools Day

Should you be following our progress you will have noticed we've just had a stroke of good luck to follow the bad we've been experiencing recently and thus morale has risen rather a lot.

The past day we've been slow, I mean seriously slow. We've been trimming and trimming and trimming desperately trying to gain more boat speed. The navigator has been meticulously studying to see if some strange current has us in it's cruel grasp and the Skipper has exhausted his extensive experience yet still, we've been dog slow.

This afternoon a friendly voice came on the VHF and to our biggest surprise it wasn't one of the Challenge fleet (well, there is no-one else out here!!).Turns out it's an Australian submarine commander who says that they've been following the race's progress with interest over the past month as they are scheduled to be in these waters for this time. Apparently they've even been watching the boats! They noticed we've been dropping back and so came over to look. They reported that we had hooked a fishing net (this is interesting as there was a big discussion a few days ago that we were too near a fishing buoy!) and were hauling a few hundred-weight of hoki! He said he thought we probably didn't want it, so cut it off and we should find things are a bit more back to normal.

We were a bit worried at this point as we thought it might constitute 'outside assistance' and we'd have to report ourselves to the race committee, but upon checking the rules there is no mention of submarines freeing fishing nets being assistance.

The commander wished us well and said they had a sweep stake running and his money was on Stelmar. Nice chap! Anyway, onward we go and you'll now see we've trucking along, kite up at about 12 knots. Wonderful!

Phil Beck & Ben Pike.
Team Stelmar – SAFE, HAPPY, FAST

Some people fell for it.

There was a bit of a debate for a while from the people that had read the log, as to whether we were cheating by receiving outside assistance.

Needless to say, there was no fishing net and no submarine, it was an April Fools Day joke.

It was quite a good log though, I must admit.

As well as the navigators spending more time below deck, so did the log writers.

I was happier on deck these days, where it was all happening.

There were three of us on Grunter watch that helmed and the same on Groaner watch, I think.

It is not easy to helm and sail a proper course, taking into account the waves and the fluctuating wind speed and direction. It was imperative that we kept the boat going as fast as possible and that doesn't always mean sailing in a straight line.

Sometimes, you have to try and take the waves at an angle to avoid literally crashing into, or off the back of a wave.

You could overtake the wave that you were sailing on and push the bow into the back of the wave in front of you, sending gallons of water cascading down the decks and effectively clearing anything in its way.

These things slowed the boat down. Some waves could easily injure the crew and put them out of action for the next time that we needed to go up.

Injured people couldn't help out.

You don't just plough through regardless.

Bearing away and speeding up make the impact harder.

We got hurt more.

What you need to do is to come up on the wind a little and slow down slightly. That way we can rush up and get the job done, whilst the boat bobs over some of these bigger chaps rather than attempting to bully its way through them.

Some helming styles were barbaric to say the least.

People would just point the boat in a straight a line as they could and smash, bash and crash the boat and its contents through whatever was coming our way.

Even when we were sent up on to the bow to work, they would just shove the front of the boat into anything with absolutely no regard for what was happening to us or the consequences for ourselves or the boat.

We talked and talked about the safest and the fastest way to sail, which included *feathering* the boat up on the wind to slow it down to about five knots when we went forwards to work in dangerous conditions.

This meant that whilst we still had enough drive to keep the boat moving and be able to get over the top of any big waves, we bobbed over them and the bow was kept relatively dry and stable.

Alex was good at this technique and used to keep a close eye on us up at the front.

We practically insisted that he take the wheel when we could, but occasionally we were out-ranked and that meant that we had a hell of a time up there.

The job then took three times as long and there were always problems.

Some people just couldn't grasp what we were trying to achieve.

Maybe they thought that they knew better or that we were being prissy.

They didn't and we weren't.

We were actually getting quite good.

Listen up.

Overnight on 2nd April the wind dropped away. The average boatspeed aboard Stelmar on the 1800 – 2200 hours watch was 2 knots. The sked however placed us only a half a mile behind Pindar.

It was still all to play for.

All we needed was some wind.

Luck was with us and the wind slowly built all day.

By mid-afternoon we had 22 knots of breeze and the flanker flying, with Stelmar chomping at the bit, achieving a maximum boat-speed of 14.5 knots.

The afternoon sked placed us 18 miles ahead of Pindar.

The relief was noticeable on Clive's whole demeanor.

Everyone aboard smiled that day.

The Southern Ocean, however, had a parting shot for us.

Overnight on the 3rd we were sailing with the wind behind us and the flanker flying when we got caught out by a gust. We went into an involuntarily gybe, pulling a block out of the foredeck which was being used as a mainsail preventer.

We gybed the kite and spent the next two hours on the foredeck as we barrelled our way towards Cape Town at all possible speed.

As dawn broke and the coast of South Africa came into view, the wind dropped away and we realised that all our efforts had been worth it.

Phil, Alex and I had finished the job of replacing the block before coming off watch, a job that could have taken hours.

We had taken 20 miles out of the leaders and we were now 74 miles ahead of Pindar.

Imagine it.Done had gone too close inshore and having lead for most of the leg, slipped back into fourth place.

The fog closed in as we approached Cape Town, which meant that the rib which Vale had organised to come out and meet us, couldn't find us.

We slipped into Cape Town on 6th April after thirty-seven days at sea, grabbing third place.

That was better.

It felt great to get a good finish.

Amidst the throng of friends and family waiting on the pontoons, my Mum and Step-father were there to greet Team Stelmar in and the usual first night party went well.

Spirits were obviously running high within the team, we were held back until the official photographs were taken and then we joined in the celebrations.

Inexplicably, I felt slightly subdued.

All the crews tended to stay by their boats and we all cheered each other in, so the party just kept on getting better as more boats arrived and more crews joined in.

I had gotten drunk when we arrived in Buenos Aires, but not in Wellington.

I didn't get drunk tonight either.

Mum and Mike were waiting with their banner and I was eventually allowed to go and hug them.

It was great to see them.

I felt far away from my previous life whilst at sea and coming ashore and seeing my family and friends was a real sight for sore eyes at every port that we visited.

Although I didn't get drunk, the Southern Ocean buzz didn't really kick in because I pretty quickly became the victim of a real humdinger of a hangover that was to last for months to come.

Tina had been due to arrive in a couple of days time.

We had been in touch via e-mail from the boat but there was nothing forthcoming from her and all conversations were one way, I thought of myself in a blood, stone, squeezing situation.

When I had asked for her flight details, she avoided answering me directly even though I persistently and directly asked.

She made a point after the start, when she was totally inconsolable, of vowing to not be around for another start or finish.

She just couldn't deal with it.

There were a great many people that were concerned for her at that time.

I was dreading it.

I was concerned that she hadn't been coping very well since then and was desperate to see her and hold her once again.

To make her laugh, to see a smile in her eyes again.

Eventually, I checked which flights were arriving from London Heathrow with the airport and was waiting at arrivals when her flight landed.

She was already crying when she walked through the doors and couldn't manage a smile.

I crossed through the waiting barrier and held her tightly.

I wanted to make all the demons leave her and let her know that she was loved.

It was a cold embrace, she was crying her eyes out and her brow was furrowed.

Something was desperately wrong.

On the journey back to Cape Town in the back of the rented car, I couldn't take in the world outside of my concentration. I held her tightly and slowly a smile spread across her face. Her eyes were dimmed though, once so bright and lively, now weak and defeated. When we got back to the bungalow that Mum & Mike had rented, they went out for a walk and left Tina and I alone.

She began crying again almost immediately and told me that she wanted to postpone the wedding, due to take place in August later that year, when I got back.

She couldn't tell me why, she told me repeatedly that she couldn't work out what was the matter and that she still loved me, just wasn't coping with the pressure and needed us to resume our life together before planning the marriage.

She nearly left on her second day, but decided that she wanted to stay in South Africa for a holiday.

She stayed for a while and eventually plucked up the courage to tell me that she wanted to call off the engagement.

She went further in fact, she was leaving Cape Town.

The next day.

I stood with her on the corner of the street waiting for the taxi to the airport, when it came I kissed her and wiped away her tears.

She got in and they drove off.

It was as easy as that.

More protests.
Vaio retired from Leg 4 due to hitting the finish mark in light winds and fail-

ing to re-cross the line. Due to a new found honesty policy on board, they notified us on 26th April.

Pindar were awarded a forty minute penalty for running their engine in reverse which placed them joint 9th place.

Amadeo Sorrentino placed a log with yachting monthly which detailed a distinct lack of harmony aboard Vaio and a desperate crew who viewed him as a tyrant and basically too passionate.

Things had come to a head in Wellington and led them to be ill prepared for this leg, seeing them finishing in 12th place before their retirement.

At the prize-giving this time we didn't fare quite so well but we did add another *First Over the Start* prize from Pindar which meant that at least some of us would get to go out on their Open 60 for a corporate day when we got back.

Quite a good prize really.

Leg 5 Cape Town to Boston

Leggers for this leg were David Hulf, Sharon Callaghan and Rob Packham.

Race re-start from Cape Town was on Sunday May 1st at 1400 hours local time.

I was really hacked off from Day One.

The spirit of adventure wasn't burning in my breast like it had been, I was dull and aching inside.

We met up for breakfast on the morning of race re-start but I couldn't eat anything so Phil ate first his, then mine.

I knew that I could depend on *Number One.*

I walked off and left them to eat.

I wandered down to the pontoons and sat on a concrete step slightly away from the boats and the well-wishers.

I wasn't ready for this leg.

Once I knew I was alone, I cried my eyes out.

Slowly the whole area started filling up with people and I tried to pull myself together before I was *busted* (Seen).

I obviously was seen before I visibly pulled myself together.

Amongst others, Julian saw me and his only comment was "Hang in there."

That was the best advice I got.

It's no good saying to a three year old child that has fallen and grazed his knees *"It doesn't hurt"* when it obviously does.

You have to work through it in your own head and that doesn't happen straight away.
Just 'hang in there'.

Thanks Julian.

We received our fleet blessing and photographs whilst Phil and I spent the entire time thinking about when we could get back to the task at hand, tying the gas bottles into place, without being obviously disinterested in the shenanigans going on alongside.

We returned to the task immediately we reasonably could, with a brief lapse of attention from Phil as the Majorettes marched by ... obviously!

The winds were light and as the starting gun was fired, the fleet drifted over the line. Stelmar were third boat off and as we approached the first laid mark, the wind filled in steadily to eventually reach twenty knots from due south.

Perfect.

Get the spinnakers up and truck along in the right direction, under stunning African skies.

(Slight smile)

We launched the race kite first, but as the breeze built, we peeled to the Flanker and we were away.
Far away from dry land and it's bitter memories.

There is a T.S.S. in place just outside Cape Town, the likes of which we were all wise to by now and this time, Challenge business routed us away from them, via a couple of designated waypoints.

Grunter watch came off at 1800 hrs (local) and we quickly established the watch system that was to be our life once more.

I couldn't eat anything so I went straight to my bunk.
I laid awake for a few hours and then received my wake-up call.
We were due back on deck for the 2200-0200 hours watch.

The wind had built to between 25-30 knots as Stelmar ploughed through the slight swell achieving a top speed of nearly 16 knots.

It was great to be sailing at night once more.
My favourite time to be sailing.

For the next four days we enjoyed spectacular conditions, the routine of kite peeling and packing, taking over our daily lives.

At the top end wind range, when we were changing down from our flanker, the boat was usually over-pressed and it was very unsteady up there on the bow. Generally there was water coming over the deck but the main difficulty that we had on the front was the roll of the boat from side to side, it was like trying to work whilst standing on the ends of a see-saw rather than the middle.

The bonus was that the *Ice cream* headaches were becoming just another bitter memory.

The water coming over the front was mild and it was actually quite pleasant getting drenched up on the bow now.

Everybody wanted to be a bowman now!

The drysuits leaked and we were soaking all the time, but the water was blue instead of grey and warm instead of cold.

It was now fun.

The nights were balmy and we wore less clothing underneath our drysuits as we worked on deck.

The sun has some serious peculiarities though.

Due to the amount of time that we have been using the various sails on the race so far, they had all been seriously weakened by not only our own tears and repairs, but also by the ultra-violet rays emitted.

With those facts in mind, we pretty much worried like a new mother over our spinnakers each time they collapsed and snapped back into shape. We chewed our fingers even further down their quick, winced, closed our eyes and clenched our buttocks.

The waves, squalls and roll of the boat mean that the wind pressure is never constant on the sails.

The sail repair team felt it more keenly than anyone.

Maybe we should have put Paddington Bear type labels on the bags *'My name is Race Kite, Please look after me?'*

The effects of the roll of the boat and the acceleration and deceleration as a result of surfing down waves and stopping at the bottom of them together with the wind squalls and lulls, means that there is a massive variation in the overall pressure on the sails, resulting in very uneven wear, tear and chaffing.

It was the job of the trimmer to try and take the sting out of the snatch by easing the sheet.

Not all of them were aware of that fact.

If a sail had a wind range of between ten and fifteen knots, and the apparent wind speed was varying between eight and twenty knots, you had to decide which sail plan to go for to achieve maximum boatspeed.

The temptation is to go for the most that you can carry, but that is not always the best approach as any damage takes time to repair and can cost you miles in the long run. Too much sail and you'll doubtless be called out of your bunk to retrieve and repair, too little sail and you would be woken with the bad news, either vocally or in interpretation of body language from the on watch crew, of the latest sked.

During the last stop-over, we had been told by the representatives from Hood's sail makers that some of our sails could be up to fifty per cent weaker than their original build strength.

We spent as much time as we could with the Hoods sail team during stop-overs, asking their opinions and getting all the help that we could from them.

They, and all the technical team from Challenge, were completely behind the race and were never too busy to offer advice or answer any questions that we had.

However ridiculous or trivial it may seem to them.

Sometimes, although for vast periods of time we were out of sight of every-one, we would encounter one or more of the other Challenge yachts.

Sometimes as blips of light in the distance getting smaller, sometimes clos-ing on us and getting bigger.

We saw them and they saw us.

There's no doubt that we were watching each other for the whole time that we were in view of each other. We were all completely focused on going faster than our competitors. We studied each other through skeds, binoculars, radar and naked eye.

Constantly.

Overnight on the 5th May, whilst Nicko was helming, we had been moni-toring one of the other Challenge yachts which we soon identified positively as BP Explorer.

We got close enough to see them in the dark.

BP's skipper, Dave Melville, was well known as an aggressive sailor and as if on cue, he began to show signs of wanting to luff us.

We were going slightly faster than them, but at a lower angle and catching them which meant that we were the overtaking/windward boat and had to keep clear of them.

We started to close on each other. In thousands of miles of open ocean, some boats are drawn to each other like magnets.

We should have sailed deeper, earlier and simply crossed behind them, passing them safely and persuing our chosen course, whilst allowing them to follow theirs.

As it was, we were converging course.

We began to talk about what we should do if we continued to close and took up the positions for first trimming the kite as we turned more on to the wind to try and avoid them and then to possibly dropping it and hoisting the headsails.

As we were flying a spinnaker, we may well have to drop it if they took us above our intended course, which under the Yacht Racing Rules, they were entitled to do as the right of way yacht.

A call came through the dark which was instantly recognizable as Dave Melville's.

"Stelmar, you've just caused me to bear away."

I replied.

"We are coming up, but you must give us opportunity to keep clear."

Silence.

As we altered our course and trimmed our sails, the apparent wind direction came forward it's speed increased and we were able to accelerate a little.

Once we had cleared them, we were ahead and we were able to bear away to our intended course thereby breaking the overlap that they had held on us.

Now that we had broken it, they were technically the overtaking boat and had to keep to a proper course, even though we were still the windward boat.

The Yacht Racing Rules and the rules for Preventing Collisions at Sea were coming into play.

I was up to speed on my knowledge of the rules, I consider.

I called out.

"We have broken the overlap, please sail your proper course."

"**** off!"

"No, you **** off!"

I knew that both his response and mine were not permitted in the rules book and perhaps unsurprisingly, Clive was on deck in a flash, still in his underwear and blinking as he tried to adjust to his night vision having literally just jumped out of his bunk.

He wasn't delighted with the language, obviously.

We sailed a higher course away from them, back into the night.

For the next couple of hours we could see their masthead light in the distance but the incident had passed and they slipped away from us.

Grrrr!

It took a week before the inevitable happened and at 0900 hours on Sunday 7th, Grunter watch were called on deck to help Groaner watch retrieve the flanker which was in shreds.

I thought we'd told you to look after it?!

Another sewing circle was formed that started the laborious task of mending it.

For the next few days, we utilized the promo and race kites, holding our breath and crossing our fingers that they would hold until we were able to fly the flanker once more.

On the morning of the 12th, the Race kite suffered a similar fate to the flanker.

At 0545 hours, just before watch change over, following the previous evenings bad sked which had seen us slip from first place to sixth, the call was made to peel the flanker in favour of the race kite.

We still had sixteen knots of breeze.

It was too windy.

Grunter watch came on deck at 0555 hours and at 0610 hours, having immediately set about gybing the boat, we shredded the race kite in fifteen and a half knots of wind.

The pattern of sewing and packing was well established as we struggled to keep an effective sail wardrobe available.

No sooner was one repaired than it was hoisted back on deck to be risked once more in an unceasing attempt to maintain maximum boat speed.

That night, I was beating myself up over what had come to light in Cape Town and couldn't sleep during my off watch from 2200-0200 hours.

I eventually got out of my bunk. The boat was sailing easily in the now light winds and life on deck was sweet.

Kate was on Mother for Groaner watch, so was below deck. She had nothing much to do, having made them all a warm drink and cleaned and scrubbed the boat all day.

Knowing that I was feeling like crap and probably looking like it too, she made me sit down and play Top Trumps with her.

I think she let me win.

I still felt the same afterwards, so we listened to her i-pod player and I chose all the sad songs, which she protested at, but let me listen to.

That didn't help either.

As a last resort, she made me put my life-jacket on and dragged me up to the foredeck, where we sat on the spinnaker bag in front of the mast.

She pointed out a few stars and constellations and then went quiet.

It was a beautifully clear night and the stars and the night sky were overwhelming.

We stared heavenward, reflecting on where we were and what we were achieving and enjoyed the moment.

That did help.

In a few moments, the first flying fish of this leg made an appearance. It hit the deck and bounced into my lap, before flapping around on the deck, spreading sales and fish oil everywhere it went.

It eventually went from whence it came, hastened by a La Chameau yachting boot.

Our moment was over, but the lesson was learned.

The magical moment was just that, a moment.

I remained pretty self-absorbed for a great deal of the leg and one day a photo of me appeared as a screen saver on the media computer.

I was my usual self and with a scowl, asked what it was doing there.

Paula replied that she had put it there.

It was, she said, a good photo of me as I looked 'approachable'.

It was a good point, well made and I made an extra effort to smile a little more often from then on.

Looking back at some photos, I discovered one of Paula and Alex together whilst I was in the background driving the boat, which was taken around this time, obviously unaware of the camera being pointed in my direction.

I was helming downwind in thirty knots of wind at times with the spinnakers straining as full as we dare let them and was concentrating like a demon.

The following waves were perfect for surfing occasionally and we exceeded twenty knots at times.

Life was good, if not a little nerve jangling.

The boat-speed was good and I was totally focused on hitting the predicted targets, but it would have been true to say that I was not exactly happy with the situation in my head.

Although the photo wasn't actually of me, it is strikingly clear that I did, in fact, produce one of the most un-approachable scowls that I have ever seen.

Small wonder then that I was steered clear of or approached with a certain amount of trepidation by some.

A few people had experienced me blowing up first hand when I had been in an apparently good mood, now I was in a foul mood, it must have made sense to approach with caution.

Later, when we crossed the finish line in Boston, Clive thanked everybody for their efforts during the leg and made a particular point of singling me out saying how well I had done in coping, as he had harboured doubts about me making it to the end.

Whether his fears were that I would have quit or someone given me a shove over the side one night, I wasn't sure.

I did make it.

**** *the Begrudgers.*

At 0020 hours the wind increased sharply to 35 knots and Groaner watch had to "jump to it" to drop the kite.

It seemed like the same old story.

We were now well rehearsed in retrieving a torn spinnaker.

Unfortunately this time, it had caught the wind during the drop and re-filled, pulling out of the crews' hands as it did so.

The lazy guy (one of the spinnaker control lines) somehow managed to wrap itself around Rob H. Rob P. and Julian, who copped the worst of it.

Julian was dragged to the end of his safety tether and pulled towards the boom with the rope wrapped around his waist and lower chest.

Alex, myself and Phil were on deck to help out in no time at all.

The lazy guy, which had snagged Julian and the others, had been cut now and the whole sail was dragging in the water behind the boat. I managed to cleat off the sheet which was still attached to the boat, whilst Julian was taken below deck for Dr. Ruth to examine him.

Julian's rope burns speak for themselves.

Ouch!

Needless to say the kite was shredded once again, the extent of which became apparent as we dragged it inch by inch back on board.

Once it was in, we continued to help on the bow, hoisting the Yankee number one and poling it out to keep Stelmar pushing through the water and maintain all possible boat speed.

At 0100 hours, we had a tea break.

Job done.

The repair to the kite was started immediately after our cup of tea.

Our leggers were settling in.

Sharon let it slip that she had a miniature bottle of whiskey which she later produced.

She had presumably brought to celebrate her birthday.

Once she realised that it was a *dry boat* with no exceptions, she had an attack of conscience and offered it as a prize on a Sunday hour long watch change-over.

We all paired up, she was quizmaster.

The usual stuff.

One of us had to count the number of questions that the other answered correctly.

Phil and I made up one team.

He counted for me and we won it.

I did feel bad for Sharon later, as I poured it over the side in an offering to King Neptune, to thank him for our safe passage thus far.

Rules are Rules and Phil and I couldn't have drunk it.

It was basically good for nothing, if you understand what I mean Neptune?

Sorry an' all that.

We crossed the equator on the 16th May and at midday watch change over as predicted, there had been some heinous crimes committed aboard that had not gone un-noticed and were therefore going to have to be a trial.

The Court of King Neptune was re-convened.

Our skipper took Neptune's role (although he dipped out on the whiskey).

Sharon, Rob Packham and David had never crossed the equator before and the opportunity to try them and punish them for their alleged crimes was seized with both hands by all the crew that had suffered a similar trial on our outbound track.

A couple of days' stale food and as much gunk that we could muster was added to the fermenting broth in the days preceding our anticipated crossing, just in case they were guilty.

We were ready for the officialdom.

They faced a full and fair trial and were found guilty in the presence of King Neptune, Queen Codface, various hecklers, henchmen, prosecution, defence lawyers and some *expert* witnesses, they were suitably punished.

The procedure was the same as the outbound crossing and involved kneeling in front of the King and Queen, surrounded by various Court Officials, with just your underpants on and getting liberally *gunked* with our pre-prepared concoction.

Sharon didn't take it too well and threw the stuff around.

It took us half an hour to clean the boat after that.

We crossed our outbound track at 2145 hours GMT on the 17th May 2005 and officially became circumnavigators by sail.

We opened a bottle of champagne and inwardly reflected on our journey so far.

Life felt good.

We finished the repair to the race kite on the 20th and proceeded in shredding the flanker on the 21st, mainly due to the fact that we were attempting to use it as a tri-radial sail in sixteen knots of wind with an apparent wind angle of eighty degrees.

More sewing required from the *Well Hard Sewing Circle*.

By now, tropical squalls and showers were being regularly monitored on the radar.

Often, somebody was posted as lookout at the nav station, constantly watching the radar screen and relaying any information regarding track, progress etc. of any clouds to those up on deck.

They showed up as blips on the radar and we could track them from about fifteen miles away.

What we couldn't do was accurately predict how close they were going to come to us and if they would hit us or not.

If they simply passed close by, we could get a little gust which would be great. You have to judge which side of it you wanted to hit so that the direction of the squall was favourable, but these boats aren't that maneuverable and sometimes you had to take what you got.

If they rolled right over the top of us, they could create mayhem.

We tracked them all around us, praying that we could make a good call before a squall hit us and we shredded another kite.

The six hourly skeds were looking good, we had been either at the front of the fleet or near to it since race start and had managed to cross the equator and get through the doldrums with little or no delay.

Things were looking so good that at one time, the fleet received an e-mail from Challenge saying "you'd better slow down; we're not ready for you in Boston yet!"

As if on cue, the wind dropped and we slowed down to a snail's pace.

It was hot and sticky aboard and some frustrating times were had by all.

Condensation below deck was a real issue and everything was leaking wet. Coupled with the lack of movement of the stagnant air and the sweaty clothes and bodies, life aboard became testing once again.

A large area of high pressure started to open up meaning that some tactical decisions were necessary. Up until now there had been plenty of wind barreling us along in the general direction of Boston, this high pressure system was directly in our path, we had to take an educated guess as to which way we tackled it to make the best headway.

The race was wide open once again.

We were good at boatspeed but our tactics had let us down up until now.

The dark clouds of the tropics were not the only ones bothering us. Now we had a dark gloom cloud hovering above us to contend with which is far worse.

The boats around us, Vaio, Spirit of Sark, Bp Explorer and Imagine it. Done all went to the west, whilst Barclays and BG Spirit went to the east and passed within sight of us. We tried a more conservative route and headed towards the middle.

As the skeds came in over the next few days, it became obvious that ours was not the winning route. BG Spirit managed to avoid the wind hole completely and were off.

The boats that favoured a more westerly route all managed to keep some wind and slowly pulled away from us.

We lost the advantage that we had held from the start and slowly dropped back down the fleet.

I submitted another daily log on the twenty-fourth of May.

Daily Log 24th May 2005

It won't change me!

As I sailed away from Gunwharf Quay,
I knew this race would not change me.
My life and love would be the same,
the day I sailed back home again.
But I learned to cook, I learned to sew,
Got called a fiery so and so.

I carried sails, as heavy as heck,
Up and down and back on deck.
The waves piled up and bore right down,
thundering loud, with deafening sounds.
Seals, Dolphins, Sharks and Whales,
All spotted as we trimmed the sails.

Heading down through warmer climes,
King Neptune punished me my crimes.
I learned about the sky at night,
Saw shooting stars and Southern Lights.
Sunsets and Rises oh! so rare,
Got dazzled in the orange glare.
In BA and later Cape Town too,
I saw some kids, that had no shoes,
In shanty towns, and rubbish tips,
They clambered over my tit-bits,
And yet they smiled so big and bright,
Eyes lit up, a special sight.

We sailed in snow and wind and hail,
Got hammered by a full force gale.
Scaled the mast and climbed the pole,
I got a glimpse of a naked soul.
Days and days, with little sleep,
Memories that are mine to keep.

In Cape Town had my hair dyed blue,
alongside all the other crew.
Was sickened deep as we turned back,
to offload a second Medivac.
Cried as my love's head was turned,
(I hope she gets her fingers burned!)

And now as we head North again,
I know my life won't be the same,
At home when I look out to sea,
Or feel the cool refreshing breeze.
Or head back in to Gunwharf Quay,
I know this race has helped me see.
Richard Parson
Team Stelmar – Safe, Happy, Fast.

Phil started taking an interest in the boat camera and was attempting to take some unusual photos. A bit more interesting than some efforts and at least he was making an effort.

One day we received a photo from Vaio. The picture was of two of the girls, one of them licking the ear of the other. It was slightly suggestive and was meant for Phil as he had been getting friendly with *the Licker*.

In response to this photo, Phil stripped off completely and held a spinnaker pole in a strategic position to cover his modesty and we sent that around the fleet.

It got better; he started taking pictures from all sorts of weird and wonderful angles and sending them around the fleet as a sort of 'Guess what this is?' type game.

His career as a photographer kind of tailed off after that but it was a fine effort.

Fun with the camera continued and one day a photo of someone's backside appeared on our media computer.

There was a 'who-dunnit?' type investigation as to whose it was.

It turned out to be Flash's. Apparently he was trying to see how badly he was affected by the condition known as Yottie Bottie.

Although he denied it, it was pretty obvious from the time it was taken, which was recognizable from the properties displayed on the computer and the glimpse of a climbing harness around his waist in the picture.

His condition was mild as far as I was concerned, so I copied him and we sent a photo of a severe case (mine) around the fleet to see whether anyone had worse.

There were no replies.

Maybe I had let the hygiene side of things slip a little.

It wasn't to do with sitting down though, had that been the case, it would have manifested itself much more seriously than it ever did.

Mostly, we were getting the idea that we were racing and therefore pushing ourselves and the boat, in order to achieve better results. On the 27th Clive asked for all people that were trimming or grinding the winches, to stand up when they were working or waiting for the bark of *Trim* or *Grind* from the person on the other end of the sheet.

He asked that we leave our teas and coffees out at the same time.

It had long been the practice that the drivers didn't have a drink until after they had finished their stint, but now we were taking it further. We were changing around positions every half an hour, so it wasn't exactly a tough thing to do.

Not tough, but seemingly difficult for some.

Ruth was admonished by Clive for sitting down when she was supposed to be working the winch, as a lot of people were now doing regularly.

Technically, they were ready as they had their hands on the winch handle, but they weren't exactly poised to grind. Their backsides were planted on the deck and no real punishment could be afforded to the winch unless you get your shoulders above it and work.

Ruth stood up but twenty seconds later was sat down again.

Clive spoke up but Ruth replied that she had a problem with one of her legs and had to sit down to rest it.

Clive had a word with Tigger and told him not to put her on grinding, there were some mutterings that she could stand at the wheel whilst helming well enough ...blah blah blah ...

We were letting the heat and the conditions get to us again.

Almost on cue, the gas situation became a concern.

We were getting through it much more quickly than we had been to date. When we got down to the last full bottle, we began to suspect that the bottles weren't fully filled in Cape Town.

By the 31st May we had run out of marmalade, jam, peanut butter, ketchup, sweet chilli sauce and coffee.

We were running out of gas and now, the sugar was low.

To conserve gas, we had to stop baking bread and there was only to be one hot drink per watch.

That took care of the situation regarding drinks on watch, but standing up whilst ready to work a winch, dozing on deck and sitting on the high side of the boat was still regarded by some as a matter of personal choice rather than team policy.

It was as if we bought into the idea of team effort, but only really verbalized it when we couldn't help ourselves but to inform everyone else of their shortcomings.

"Sleeping is for wimps!" came Newton's comment, one that would have made me choke on my *nice cup of coffee* had there been enough gas to boil the kettle.

There wasn't enough gas though and we had to finish this leg yet.

We were still about a week away from finishing and the forecast was for a bit of a blow in the next few days.

The feelings that you have, waiting for the wind to really blow imminently, is intense.

Other than the pettiness of living in the contained environment with seventeen other people, the weather rules your life.

More accurately, the forecast governs your concerns.

At 0730 hours on the 1st June, the predicted freight train ran through, with a maximum gust of 47 knots blowing from 233 degrees.

Perfect, for reaching.

Dead Fast.

A bit bumpy though.

We had two reefs in the main and the number two yankee up. The storm staysail was hanked on ready to fly and replace the yankee and maybe even the main, if the breeze continued to build.

The sea-state was building and we were ready and waiting.

I was spared my *Mother Watch.*

David Hulf had taken my spot below whilst I was seconded to enjoy the conditions on deck.

Yippee!

Sue was whittering on about some log amendment that I had posted that had upset her, so to be below deck with her when she was awake, would have been torment in the extreme for me.

I was freed to go on deck and help sail the boat.

She moaned to anyone that would listen, whilst I was on deck, sailing the boat as best as I could.

'Frankly my dear, I don't give a damn!'

Blow wind, blow!

A few days later, the daily log described how the leggers were coping with life aboard.

The core crew tried extremely hard to make the leggers fit in but there were some glaring differences in our general demeanour around the boat.

Sharon was having difficulties finding her feet and wrote this log on 4th June, it sums it up well I think.

<u>Daily Log 04th June</u>

You Know You're A Legger When…

It takes 20 minutes to wrestle yourself into your mid layer, foulies and wellies by which time the rest of the crew have eaten and are on their way up for watch change…

When the helm shouts 'wave' you look up while everyone else ducks…

You use the 'wrong' loo when heeled over and spend 15 minutes pumping out the evidence…

You put your tea / food down without noticing that everyone is cradling theirs – whoosh, there goes your portion decoratively worn by a fellow crew member…

You stagger around like a drunk on a binge, trying to keep up with those nonchalant souls who appear to move effortlessly from one end of the boat to the other…

You always seem to be clipped onto the place that never quite lets you reach where you need to be working…

After a two-day hunt, you eventually find your recently washed pants underneath a sail that weighs more that you do…

You STILL can't remember which way is clockwise round the winch…. "No the OTHER clockwise…"

6 new bruises appear daily and you've no idea where they came from…

You know you've 'made it' when…

Your heart rate doesn't race when asked to 'gybe the kite'...

You ask for seconds of rehydrated potato and beef stew in a bag...

The sail change goes smoothly despite 45-knot gusting winds and lumbering under water on the bow...

After kneading bread at a 45-degree angle at three a.m., two delicious brown loaves emerge from the oven...

You have sailed over 6000 miles, seen dolphins, whales and waterspouts and feel part of a team travelling safe, happy and fast...

Sharon Callaghan, David Hulf and Rob Packham
Team Stelmar 'Leggers' – Safe, Happy and Fast

Needless to say, the humour helped them get on with the rest of us. They were getting the hang of sailing as well, if the truth be known.

Good job too, we were nearly there.

In the meantime, the wind had come forward and we were facing a high pressure system which effectively blocked our way.

We had to go to one side or the other of it, or else stop in the middle where there is no wind to speak of.

We went to the north of it.

It was a gamble that didn't pay.

BG group had run straight to the north, they went as far as they dare and pulled out an eventual 300 mile lead on the second place boat.

We sort of copped out half way through and got stuck, whilst most of the fleet went to the south and maintained some kind of forward momentum.

After 36 days, 16 hours, 2 minutes and 46 seconds we crossed the finish line by the Boston Harbour Hotel having slipped back to eighth place.

A launch chartered by some of our family and friends came out to meet us and threw over some beers, we made our way over to the moorings of the hotel and joined the rest of the fleet.

We got ashore just after midnight and the champagne corks were popped as we joined the party ashore.

Unfortunately, drinking in public is illegal in Boston after 2.00am so it was a short-lived party there.

We made our way to the accommodation once we were refused service, some of us with bottles hidden away.

The party continued in the accommodation but I sat outside on a bench with a bottle of champagne and no company.

I wasn't being rebellious over the drinking laws, it's just that a full-on streamers and balloons party would have killed me, I think.

I just sat there on my own, with a bottle of booze and a packet of cigarettes and stared at the sea.

Protests in Boston...

On 11th June, the International Jury heard a protest regarding an alleged incident between BP Explorer and Unisys/EMC2 and a luffing incident after dark.

The results of the hearing were explained the following way;

The results of the protest have been received, and the International Jury have found against BP Explorer.

The international jury convened Saturday at 10.00 am the panel consisted of 5 jurors from 3 nationalities (2 Americans, 2 Canadians & 1 British Juror). Having established the validity of the protest the jury then heard from both parties and their nominated witnesses with the arguments and cross examinations lasting for a total of approximately 2 1/12 hours. The jury then spent a further 2 hours deliberating the facts before reaching a final decision.

As we explained previously, the case essentially revolves around the fact that the fleet races under 2 sets of rules. During the hours of daylight from Sunrise until Sunset the Racing Rules of Sailing apply, after Sunset and before Sunrise the IRPCAS (International Regulations for Preventing Collisions at Sea) apply. In this case the incident happened 40 minutes after Sunset - therefore the IRPCAS rules were those in force, specifically Rule 17.

*Whilst a racing sailor's natural instinct is to defend his or her position on the race course, this cannot be done after Sunset without consideration for the restrictions imposed by IRPCAS. **BP Explorer's** actions were therefore a technical infringement of the rules and as such **Imagine It. Done.** were correct to bring to the matter before the international jury. The international jury having upheld the protest and penalised **BP Explorer** 3 points. In accordance with General Sailing Instruction 22, the positions and points of other boats will remain unchanged. The international jury's decision is final and not open to appeal.*

Having been luffed at night by BP Explorer ourselves, there was a certain amount of hand rubbing in the Stelmar camp.

Hard luck BP.

Tee! Hee!

At the prize-giving in Boston we picked up the 24 hour run prize again but this time we (Julian mainly) had been working hard on the safe bit of our objective and we won the BP Safety Award for the leg.

Safe and Fast.

Boston to La Rochelle

We left Boston on 19th June. There was the usual blessing of the fleet and group photographs before we slipped dock.

For this leg, Mike True, Adrian MacMahon and Primrose Keenan joined us as leggers. Primrose had been in Portsmouth back in October so was well known to us in the team, as was Adrian who worked for Stelmar/OSG and had been involved with the project since the sponsors were announced. It was Adrian, in fact, that presented us with the St. Nicholas medal (St. Nicholas is the patron saint of sea-farers) many months previously, which hung in the galley and had done a good job of looking over us since that time.

Mike was an experienced sailor who had competed in the Challenge Business Round Britain and Ireland Race, so was welcomed as a competent and regarded sailor.

The wind was light as we headed out towards the starting area prior to our third Atlantic crossing.

A feature of the early stages of this leg was going to be the Labrador Current which flows down from Newfoundland bringing cold water with it and occasionally icebergs.

Our rough game plan was to head north early and try to locate ourselves on the southernmost part of the North Atlantic low pressure system and the northernmost part of the Azores high pressure system.

That way, we could hopefully get the full advantage of a following breeze (and plenty of it) and we could go slightly higher for more breeze if we wanted it, or lower for less if we needed that.

The risk was the extra distance that we would have to travel to place ourselves to the north of the fleet.

We had been getting some serious weather advice.

OSG had agreed to forgo some of the crew meals in port and spend the money on better (and more expensive) weather routers

Things certainly felt better aboard, it was as if the penny had finally dropped.

We were the first boat over the line again, but this time, we were too eager and were premature in starting. Technically *On Course Side* (OCS) so we had to accept a penalty from the race committee.

The wind dropped away and by the 1800-2200 watch on the first night, the wind was blowing due east but at only 4 knots ... with lulls.

We were achieving between 1-2 knots of boatspeed and it was foggy, damp and cold.

The constant need for boatspeed is frustrating in these conditions.

Most of us tried as hard as we could to sail in the right direction with any speed that we could find, but the wind just kept dropping away or changing direction and the boat needs more attention in these conditions than it does in the harshest conditions that we had faced so far.

On 21st, things got to me again when Newton and Paula were dozing on deck, leaving Primrose to trim the kite on her own, after just three days aboard and with a maximum of two hours instruction on how to do it.

I complained to Alex my watch leader, he reported that he was 'happy with the situation'.

There was more interest in the debate of whether to call *Trim* or *Wind* when asking the person on the winch to work than there seemed to be in applying ourselves to the task of staying awake whilst on watch.

The main culprit was Alex who wouldn't let it go. He was insistent that the correct term was 'wind' when most other people thought that the call should be 'trim' which is what we had been saying so far. Newton checked the sail trim text book that we had aboard and it said the call should be trim. Alex wasn't convinced and he kept arguing with anybody that would bite.

Nicko eventually settled it with his (shared) observation by saying 'JUST WORK YOU ******'

The other bad news was that we had inadvertently bought filter coffee instead of the instant stuff that we were geared up for. We had bought chilli sauce without any chilli in it and our daily ration of chocolate bars had remained the same in number, but had been reduced to miniature sized versions.

Maybe we had been living too well and the food order was a considered one, but it caused a few questions to be asked.

Ruth blamed Flash.

Flash didn't give a **** and he probably had the right attitude.

By the 23rd we were still making very little progress and had only covered 600 miles.

We had been working hard on the sail changes and trimming but the wind was still too light to make any decent progress. The fog was a regular feature and remained with us for a couple of days as it rolled in and out of our world.

We spotted a whale and some dolphins but as dusk was settling just after the 1800 hours watch change over, in a period without any fog, Julian spotted a sailing yacht going the other way.

It had a distinct maroon coloured hull and was not one of the Challenge yachts.

He decided to try and make contact.

He brought one of the two handheld VHF radios up on deck and transmitted the following;

'Maroon yacht on our port bow, this is yacht Stelmar, are you receiving? Over.'

He was startled however by the following response;

'Maroon coloured yacht, this is yacht Stelmar, we are receiving you. Over.'

Paula had been awake below deck and had answered Julian's call on the handheld radio by using the radio at the Nav station below deck.

Peanut!

As we woke to come on deck for the 0200-0600 hours watch, I slowly became aware that the boat was rolling and pitching in the sea.

We had found some wind.

Delighted, I got on deck as quickly as I could to find that we had 23 knots of breeze and were averaging 14 knots of boatspeed.

As the mist and fog cleared, seven other Challenge yachts came into view.

The sked placed us pretty much all in the same area, with the exception of Saic/ La Jolla who had taken a more southerly route and had drawn a 75 mile lead on the rest of the pack.

It didn't matter though, we were all moving in the fresh breeze now and we were confident of our tactics.

By Sunday 26th June we were sailing in 20-25 knots of breeze from 220 degrees with the flanker up and maintaining 12 knots average boatspeed, it was fantastic.

At watch change-over, we all ate together on deck and as we had passed within 25 miles of where the Titanic was lost, Flash delivered an informative talk on that disaster and we held a two minute silence in remembrance of the 1,500 people that lost their lives there.

The lunchtime sked on Monday put us in first place with Me 2 You just one mile behind us and then a gap of 10 miles to the next boat.

Adrian, who was on Mother watch poked his head out of the companionway with the days supply of chocolate, which had been in short supply, as I mentioned.

The scene that followed was classic comedy.

Ruth, who was perched next to the wheel, practically leapt the entire length of the cockpit to get to her share.

If she had head-butted Newton, punched Phil and kicked Paula in her desperate attempt to get there, she couldn't have appeared more desperate to get some chocolate.

I wrote a couple of more logs, not many but this was one of them.

Daily log 29th June.

There's an undercurrent flowing aboard Team Stelmar at the moment.

Now you may not be surprised to hear that, since we're somewhere near the Gulf Stream in the North Atlantic on a sailing boat, whilst taking part in a yacht race, but I'm not talking about that kind of current.

No, the current that I'm talking about concerns an unspoken sentiment, maybe even a grudge, which is being harboured (do you see the nautical link?) and cultivated, amongst the crew.

The reason?
Fun sized chocolate rations.

Due to restrictions in importing foodstuffs into the U.S. it was necessary to purchase all our food for this leg in Boston, whereas nearly all our previous food was purchased and packed in the U.K. back in September 2004. This situation is certainly workable. We have planned and practically executed a complete circumnavigation by sail, with all the logistical problems which that involves.

To tackle the provisioning issue in Boston, we assigned our two most dedicated and unashamed chocoholics to the task.

What did they come back with?

FUN SIZED BARS.

I have to tell you that there is nothing fun about the size of these meager portions.
Even the most delicate of nibbles is enough to polish off a complete snack in one go.

149

When I'm in charge, fun sized will be double giant sized.

These things are hardly worth the paper they're wrapped in. They probably don't weigh much more and are really only enough to frustrate you into wishing that you had some chocolate.

From the country that brought us the biggest wrestlers, the biggest trucks, the tallest buildings, the grandest canyon and the biggest burgers, I expected better things.

I'm not angry, I'm just disappointed.

If you're coming to Portsmouth later this month, do us all on Team Stelmar a favour and stop off at a Cadburys, Mars or Galaxy shop.

Ignore the fun size and go for the double giant size.

You'll have a friend for life.

Rich Parson.
Safe, Happy, Fast.
    (That log did me a lot of good when we got to La Rochelle and later, Portsmouth too.)

    We were making good progress and on Tuesday 28th June, a predicted cold front came through and the wind picked up to 20-25 knots from the north meaning our progress was right down the line.
    Although life on deck was a constant thrill with the fresh winds and decent boat speeds, we had to laugh at Newton who was on Mother watch and was supposed to be waking the Groaners to come up on deck for the 2000-0200 hours watch.
    The trouble was, he had fallen asleep himself and wasn't going to be waking anyone.
    We even toyed with the idea of allocating someone to be responsible for making sure Newton was awake.
    Bailing out the basement while there are holes in the roof.

    The wind blew steadily for the next few days and we dropped the flanker in favour of the poled out yankee once it got above 30 knots.
    We surfed some waves and got everybody involved in sailing the boat, or at least thinking about it.
    We achieved a distance run of 269 miles on Thursday 30th June and we

regularly exceeded 20 knots of boatspeed during that period, reportedly displacing 22,000 litres of water per second as we did so.

It was becoming increasingly obvious that Mike (True) wasn't really gelling with his watch mates. Often, when I came on deck, the rest of Groaner watch were sat huddled in the rear quarter of the transom in an attempt to counter the heeling moment of the boat in some small way, Mike was usually sat near the companionway on his own.

I often tried talking to him, with limited success, but he did confide in me that he was toying with the idea of getting off in La Rochelle. He didn't elaborate on his reasons.

The sailing was absolutely fantastic at this time, so whatever it was that was bugging him, it couldn't have been that. The man that hates that feeling would hate most things.

I couldn't help him.

It may have seemed a bit late in the day as far as the race was concerned, but we started actually thinking about crew weight distribution on deck as well as below and acting on it.

It was common practice to have the off watch sleeping 'on the high side' to counter the heeling moment of the boat in some small way, but we now had the bit between our teeth and started applying the same lesson to the crew on deck.

As the wind was invariably coming from the starboard quarter, we assembled all the crew that were not actively working, into a tight group and sat them all huddled together in the same spot at the back of the boat to help in the same way.

It may have given us only a tiny percentage of boat speed advantage, but it also helped to concentrate peoples' minds on the task at hand.

Every twenty minutes, we had to remind someone to get back into position and stay where they were required.

Two or three people would slowly make their way forward again to a more comfortable spot, under the guise of having to visit the heads, or write the daily log. Anything they could think of really to move away from where they knew they should be.

They moved forward, we asked them to move back.

They argued or protested and gave some half-baked theory as to why they were better off where they were.

They moved back and then, slowly started creeping forward again immediately.

The reasons had to be explained to nearly everyone, some a few times, to get them to consider doing this. Those that were still completely in the dark as to the theory of balance and trim, were the biggest culprits, they wouldn't take kindly to being asked to do something. They knew everything by now.

Sometimes I thought that the only way to get people to sit on the windward side was to say 'Oh look, there's a dolphin!'

The fact that a couple, usually the most obstinate and selfish, couldn't tell you which side of the boat was the 'high side', couldn't tie a basic bowline knot and were totally foxed about how to go about most of the simple procedures that we employed on a daily basis after thirty-thousand miles of sailing, was irrelevant.

Just a couple of people really, but they were nigh on impossible to speak to sometimes.

Phil got it right, he just bellowed at them so that they rocked in their yachting boots.

They listened to him.

We persevered and basically kept on at everyone to sit in the correct place until they did what was right for the boat, which eventually paid dividends.

The boat speeds crept up in direct relation to the wind speed and wave height and we regularly got Stelmar rushing through the water at speeds in excess of twenty knots.

We were cooking on gas.

We were first place yacht, steaming across the Atlantic with fantastic boat speeds.

According to Nicko, when we exceeded twenty knots of boat-speed, Stelmar was displacing twenty-two thousand litres of water per second.

That's a lot of spray!

My 39th birthday was on Saturday July 2nd and at the midnight watch change over, all the crew sang happy birthday. I received three cards, all of which had the photo of my backside on the front, with various comments relating to it which were then posted on the notice board alongside the 6 hourly skeds.

Somebody had made the gooiest chocolate 'cake' that I have ever seen and having a slight penchant in that direction, I've seen a few.

We shared it at the midday watch change over, but we were within reach of a first place finish with a 20 mile lead on Unisys who were in second place. The wind was likely to drop off as we approached the coast.

I enjoyed my birthday.

Everyone always made a big effort to help each other enjoy their day and the cake and the song were appreciated, but there were 'special circumstances' in this case and we had a race to win.

The day went on with the wind blowing from 120 degrees apparent angle at about 20 knots.

We were achieving good boat speeds and the day was a good one, but we had other boats breathing down our necks.

Clive had asked if there was anything in the medical box that could help him stay awake near the end of the leg into Boston.

There wasn't.

We made provisions for this leg.

He usually stayed awake for the twenty-four hours leading up to the finish of each leg, but really did himself and us no favours by being so tired. He would create mayhem by suddenly running up on deck, after spending hours staring at the navigation computers and call for changes in everything from sail trim to wardrobe and would have us running around like demented souls whilst he wound himself and us up tighter and tighter. If there was ever the potential for conflict it was when he came on deck in a tiz, after no sleep and having received a bad sked because of it.

We decided to obtain some Pro-Plus Caffeine pills for this leg and the next one.

Alex decided to try some, for no particular reason other than to experiment with speeding his nuts off. He took about three of these tablets in one go and was absolutely manic for days. He was literally climbing the rigging at one point but was rewarded in his first attempt at controlled drug misuse with a strained shoulder and derision from those of us that were more calculating about these matters.

The Pro-Plus were relegated to his wash kit (alongside his hair gel) although judging by his behaviour he still popped a few in secret.

Both he and Phil were getting the gel ready and practicing their hairstyles for their adoring public.

The tension was high.

True to form, the wind dropped off as we neared the finish.

The headache was that it was still blowing from behind us which meant that the boats that were following us still had plenty of wind.

As we neared the finish we could see a couple of them through our binoculars. They were still behind us, but they were flying their flankers in plenty of wind whilst we were creeping along in the lightest of winds with our lightest kite barely pulling the boat along.

Aaargh!

We held our nerve though and we crossed the finish line in first place on July 4th.

American Independence Day, OSG/Stelmar were delighted.

So were we.

Phil had donned his video camera that mounts inside his sky-diving helmet and the footage that he took secured us the prize for the best video clip of the leg.

I was sitting on the side of the boat when we finished and Wrighty came over to give me a hug. I fell over backwards and everyone took it as a sign to 'pile on'.

The mass of bodies all piled on top of one another, with arms and legs flailing all over the place also housed some of the broadest smiles to date.

It was a fantastic feeling to be in first place at last, our little pill boy actually began to cry, feelings were running high and we were absolutely delighted with ourselves and our performance.

It had all come together for us at last for us.

We had put in a sterling performance and kept our heads when the pressure was on and the fleet around us were beginning to close the gap.

Unfortunately, once we had finished, the tide was out at La Rochelle and we couldn't get in to the inner harbour until it was.

We had to wait outside until there was enough water under the keel to physically get in to the harbour.

We tidied the boat and packed all the sails away in preparation for the dockside party and when we did motor in people were lined along the harbour walls, shouting, cheering and waving at us.

One person called out to welcome Mike Morgan in. He had left the boat in Buenos Aires but had obviously not told everyone.

Once we were safely moored up in the inner harbour, Clive, Wrighty, Nicko, Julian and the Pill Boy all jumped into the water.

Sunglasses sank, but the crew did not I'm pleased to report.

There's a few pounds worth of kit lying at the bottom of every stop-over port that we visited I'll bet.

I took the photos in La Rochelle, due to a complete lack of enthusiasm for that job from our *in-charge* Media Officer.

Later, when we entered the marquee bar that Challenge had set up for us, all of the other crews gave us a standing ovation.

The feeling of camaraderie amongst the fleet was tremendous and was never more obvious than at that moment.

Needless to say, we partied hard that day and we staggered home in the early hours.

Sure enough, a few days before we were due to leave La Rochelle, Mike True quit. There wasn't a great deal of surprise amongst the crew as he had discussed the matter with myself and Paul and in turn, I had spoken to Wrighty, his watch leader, and Clive to tell them what I knew.

The positive result of this was an e-mail from Challenge business to anyone that had done legs, to offer a place for the finishing leg.

J.C. was just leaving his office on Friday and was a little later getting away than normal. He checked his e-mail before intending to switch off his computer and go home, only to discover the correspondence. He jumped at the chance to get back on board; he rocked up in La Rochelle and re-joined us.

J.C. was an extremely well liked guy and we were delighted to see him again.

Phil's headcam had secured us the best video clip award but we also won the 1st place yacht on that leg and we partied hard at the prize-giving.

La Rochelle to Portsmouth.

Race re-start was on July 13th.

Although we meant to be conservative on the line because of a foul tide and the possibility of having to re-cross it to start correctly if we were premature in starting, we were over cautious.

We were too timid and were the last boat away.

There was a gate for us to pass through though and most of the boats gybed to cross through it early.

We stood on a little longer and the wind backed in our favour.

Lady Luck was with us and the changed direction put us in the perfect position to get through.

Team Stelmar was then first through the gate.

Pompey here we come, with our month's supply of Pro-plus and a thirst that'd make a brewery rich!

'NO SLEEP 'TIL POMPEY!'

Although we had 12-15 knots from the south east, the forecast was for really light winds.

The professionals that were advising us forecast *Gradient Zero* breeze for late on Thursday, but at sunrise on Paula's birthday, we were still enjoying 20 knots of it.

True to the forecast though the breeze dropped off gradually all day and by the time the Grunters came off watch at midday it had dropped away to just over 10 knots.

We ate lightly and hardly slept.

Six hours later we were back on deck going slowly in very light air.

It was going to be a slow finish.

Adrenaline and inactivity are not good bed fellows.

The course to the finish still hadn't been confirmed by Challenge because of the forecasted light conditions.

We were expected home at sometime around 1400 hours on Saturday 16th July because a lot of the sponsors, media, friends and family wanted to be there.

Because of the forecast, it was almost impossible to tell how many miles we would be able to cover over the next three days, therefore, Challenge were announcing the waypoints along the way as they monitored the state of play and therefore were governing the miles we had to cover.

They had plenty of waypoints as options, one of which was the Eddystone lighthouse, 16 miles off Plymouth Hoe.

It was the one place in the world that I longed to see.

The waypoints were always announced in a manner that wouldn't favour anyone as far as position in the fleet was concerned, maybe as far as positioning for the next little bit of breeze that came through, but they were extremely difficult to predict by anyone, so it was fair.

Fair, but unfortunate for Dave Melville and the crew aboard BP Explorer.

They had inadvertently missed out rounding a buoy just outside La Rochelle and had to turn back to go around it in the light winds that were a feature of this leg. It cost them dearly and must have been a huge disappointment to all aboard.

Especially as the eyes of the world seemed to be on us.

They were a long way behind the fleet.

As I came up on watch on the morning of Thursday 14th, the VHF radio crackled to life and I could clearly hear the sound of two Cornish fishermen chatting over the airwaves. I was looking forward to seeing the Eddystone lighthouse, which I had been hoping to see on our return track for ten months now. I hadn't bargained on the feeling of euphoria that I felt when I heard these two yapping away.

They couldn't possibly realize the feelings that they had stirred in me, they were probably totally unaware that I heard them and for them it was just another summer's morning.

For me it was the pinnacle of my race.

For me, it was as natural as liking the sound of my mother's voice.

I wanted to cry.

We continued to hear various voices and sounds throughout the day, I swear that even the seagulls seemed to possess a *Janner* burr and at 1932 hours on Friday, we rounded the Eddystone Lighthouse.

It was a beautiful summers evening and with the binoculars pressed tightly to my eyes, I could see my hometown clearly.

I picked out all the landmarks that I knew so well and thought of how it would be to return there and remembered how it was when I left.

If I could have sneaked back to my flat un-noticed, I may well have.

For me, I had succeeded in achieving my lifelong dream at that point.

The days of my childhood when the infamous Eddystone lighthouse seemed so far away and so important to me, came flooding back.

From here I could clearly see where I lived, where I was born, where I learned to sail and where some of my family still worked and lived.

I could see my primary school where we had learned all about the various lighthouses that have stood on that spot since Winstanley's first one back in 1698, built to mark the reef and offer safe guidance to shipping for the Devonport Royal Dockyard.

It was now my lighthouse and my city and it had been waiting for me.

I imagined looking out of my bedroom window at night, as I had so many times in the last year, the difference was that I would soon be able to do just that, only from now on, instead of imagining looking back into the window from the sea, I would now look out of the window at night, see the moon and imagine being at sea.

The world hadn't changed, but I seemed to have done.

Slowly the fleet made their way up the English Channel, at night we could see each others mast-head lights which served to keep us focused on getting to the Needles as quickly as we could in the meager breeze that we were experiencing.

Lobster pots, fishing boats and various different forms of shipping were crowding us out in the busy shipping area that is The Channel.

We kept going all night on Friday, aided by our Pro-plus caffeine tablets and as the dawn light broke through on Saturday morning we inched our way through the gap that is the Needles and the approach to the Solent.

The foul tide was ripping through and we all tried as hard as we could to get through the narrowest point.

There were boats all around us and positions kept changing all morning as one boat would make a little progress and then get stuck again as someone else caught a zephyr of breeze for a brief period and inched forward, only to fall into a wind hole or fall foul of the tide once more.

As we approached the Isle of Wight, our supporters boat came to rendezvous.

We all painted our faces in the blue and white colours of Stelmar/OSG and then we saw them.

There they were, at last.

Our nearest and dearest.

Funnily enough, they only stayed for a short period and then made their way back up towards Southampton Water and the finishing area.

We wondered if that was all we were going to see of them until we hit the pontoons, but it turned out that they had been taken back to watch a display by the Cadburys Bi-plane which was looping the loop etc. by way of a welcome home for the first boat back.

It was sponsored by NewNet, one of Team Stelmar's business sponsors.

They were welcoming BG Spirit in.

I know that BG won, but we were NewNet's prodigy.

C'mon guys!

OSG/Stelmar took out a half page advert in the special race edition of the Portsmouth Post.

The supporters' boat made it's way back, to track us up through the Solent in the stifling heat of the day and watched as we gybed inside Me to You just short of the finish line, pipping them at the post.

We had completed a 36,000 mile circumnavigation by sail and beaten another boat right on the line.

Our friends and family cascaded chocolate onto our decks and we had a group hug aboard as we sailed along with all our sails up and no-one in the slightest bit concerned about sail trim or even steering the boat.

We had to wait briefly as each of the previous boats made their way into Gunwharf Quays to the sounds of their selected boat songs and balloons and streamers filled the air.

A Royal Naval Minesweeper, H.M.S. Shoreham escorted us to Gunwharf whilst we were mesmerized by the amount of people that were shouting, cheering and crying on the waters edge, almost like they had been waiting for ten months.

There was a significant difference this time though, there were no long faces ashore, they were all absolutely delighted.

The atmosphere was electric.

We moored up and leapt onto the pontoons to hug and kiss the two people that we were each allowed to invite down to the boats.

There was a genuine concern that if everybody came down, the pontoons would be seriously unstable because of the combined weight, so most people were held up on the quayside.

When I did make my way up, there were the two dozen people that I had missed so much and it was all I could do to keep my composure.

We hugged, laughed, kissed and made our way to the bar.

The rest of the day was time off.

The prize-giving was due to take place on the following afternoon so we all went our separate ways.

That evening there was a big party in one of the night clubs but I had already decided that I wasn't going to attend it.

I wanted to be with my friends exclusively, not somewhere between Team Stelmar and everyone that had come to welcome me home.

We went out for a steak and some beers and afterwards, some of my closest friends came back to my little room with a view on Spice Island which I had stayed in 10 months earlier.

We drank wine and hugged each other.

At the prize-giving on Sunday afternoon Team Stelmar won a special award from Hood Sail Makers for the best on-board sail repair, another 24 hour run record and the overall fastest boat in the race.

It was a subdued affair for me and the day was really hot and still.

I shuffled about uncomfortably in the heat, as did most of us I suppose.

BG Spirit won the race overall, they deserved to do so with their solid, consistent performance.

I had wanted to win and I wasn't really that vocal when it came to cheering for them but everybody else that was there more than made up for my lack of effort and I do congratulate them.

We were 6th out of 12.

Mid fleet.

Average.

Afterwards, I went back to my room alone.

I clambered over the entire contents of my kit bags, which had been strewn across virtually the whole floor-space, making the most of having all that room to spread out in and I made my way out on to the veranda where I sat at the table and stared at the sea as the sun went down.

I drank from one of the same glasses that I had used all that time ago and reflected on the last four years, until I couldn't stay awake any longer.

Still I wasn't cold.

Still I dreamed of adventures at sea.

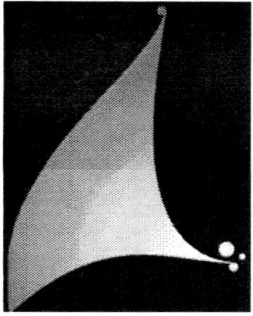